QUALITY TIME?

THE REPORT OF THE
TWENTIETH CENTURY FUND
TASK FORCE ON PUBLIC TELEVISION

with Background Paper by Richard Somerset-Ward

1993 ◆ The Twentieth Century Fund Press ◆ New York

The Twentieth Century Fund sponsors and supervises timely analyses of economic policy, foreign affairs, and domestic political issues. Not-for-profit and nonpartisan, the Fund was founded in 1919 and endowed by Edward A. Filene.

Library of Congress Cataloging-in-Publication Data

Somerset-Ward, Richard
    The report of the Twentieth Century Fund Task Force on the Future of Public Television: with background paper "Public Television: The Ballpark's Changing" / by Richard Somerset-Ward.
        p.   cm.
    Includes index.
    ISBN 0-87078-354-8 : $9.95
    1. Public television--United States.   2. Television programs, Public service--United States.   3. Public television--United States--Finance.   4. Television broadcasting--United States--Technological innovations.   I. Twentieth Century Fund. Task Force on the Future of Public Television.   II. Title.
HE8700.79.U6S66   1993
384.55'06'573--dc20   93-17145
                                                                                       CIP

Cover Design and Illustration: Claude Goodwin
Manufactured in the United States of America.
Copyright © 1993 by the Twentieth Century Fund, Inc.

QUALITY TIME?

FOREWORD

New technologies are revolutionizing global media and communications. Many believe that those institutions that fail to adapt will simply perish. Market forces, of course, will determine most of the winners and losers in the new media order, but governments must decide whether commercial forces alone will provide for the needs of their citizens. The future of American public television, in particular, will be highly dependent on the policies of the public sector.

At the heart of questions about the present and future role of public television in the United States lies a peculiarly American dilemma. While other nations always have relied heavily upon governmental support for television programming (indeed, in many cases actually barring commercial alternatives), in the 1940s and 1950s Americans allocated the available over-the-air channels in such a way that the system is overwhelmingly privately owned. This approach reflected, among other things, a basic American idea about journalism and media: that whatever its faults, the marketplace has one great virtue when it comes to providing support for the sources of news and information—it frees them from financial dependence upon government or party. Of course, it is also true that the market does not capture many values that we hold dear. What sells is seldom the same as what constitutes anyone's notion of a cultured and thoughtful society. The term "mass media" explicitly suggests the lowest-common-denominator approach of most commercial television.

When this market-driven approach to programming is combined with the current superficiality of much public affairs reporting, the result is a near obsession (through polls and ratings) with the sheer numbers of public participation, audience, and preferences. In our society, it often seems that the notion that elites in art, the professions, media, and politics have influence far out of proportion to their numbers is tolerated only as an imperfection, a sign, perhaps, that we have not achieved the true democratic ideal. The concept of media designed to lead in the debate about ideas or even to promote culture or good taste makes many politicians, not to mention sales executives, uneasy; it even can seem vaguely un-American. After all, the United States is the happy product of the marriage of democracy and capitalism. As such, it is the model for the world. In this sense, television dominated by advertising, slapstick, and gossip is a small price to pay for freedom from government fiat and, perhaps just as importantly, for a continuing emphasis on the assumed tastes of the common man.

Still, in the early years of television, voices were raised in protest because diversity of ownership had done little to ensure variety of programming and, more subjectively, even less to support quality. In this context, the development of noncommercial alternatives was supported and tolerated as a mild correction to the market-driven necessity for the three major networks to appeal to a very large portion of the population. Public television, then, was always an exception. The share of its budget provided by governments also was an expedient, a stopgap that satisfied no one completely. The system of more than 350 channels that has grown from these uncertain beginnings has contributed much to American life. But it has never found a firm basis for continuing federal support or for explicit national recognition that it plays an essential role in public discourse.

Given these fragile roots, it is scarcely surprising that support and policy direction for public television from Washington has been inconsistent and controversial. And today, when the reality of multichannel cable systems, VCRs, and even interactivity are demolishing the old market realities that shaped the development of television, both public television's friends and enemies often seem uncertain about what, if any, role it should play in the future.

In this context, the Twentieth Century Fund decided to sponsor a task force on the future of public television. Our brief is the development of public policy writ large, including the news and information businesses that shape public perception of issues. We see the future of public television as a cross-cutting issue. The small but very special component of the national resources devoted to serving the public's right to know is not only a subject of congressional and presidential policymaking, but also a topic of heated public and media debate. Perhaps the most astonishing thing about the system is its youth, for it is a mere twenty-five years since the first Carnegie Commission report laid the foundation for public television as we know it. Such a span would be only the first phase for a great newspaper, a baby step for a center of learning. Yet in the world of broadcast media, a quarter century can be more than time enough for explosive growth, brief maturity, and a rapid descent to the scrap heap. In this sense, television, both commercial and public, is ripe for, if not complete reinvention, at least creative recycling.

All this is by way of saying that we asked a lot of our Task Force members. They brought varying degrees of expertise and experience to the table. And they were asked to work through difficult and ambiguous issues of financing, quality, and public policy. The members of our Task Force represent no one but themselves; they are, in this sense, an exercise in collective citizenship. We, the Trustees and staff of the Twentieth Century Fund, believe that this group represents the best kind of intellectual—and very American—quest. We thank the members for their time and their commitment, especially the group's extraordinary chairperson, Vartan Gregorian. We think that their efforts are sure to arouse spirited debate not just about what is best for public television, but in a larger sense about what is best for the nation.

Richard C. Leone, PRESIDENT
The Twentieth Century Fund
June 1993

CONTENTS

MEMBERS OF THE TASK FORCE

Vartan Gregorian, *Task Force Chair*
President, Brown University

Peter A. A. Berle
President and CEO, National Audubon Society

David W. Burke
Vice President and Chief Administrative Officer, Dreyfus Corporation

Joseph A. Califano, Jr.
Chairman and President
Center on Addiction and Substance Abuse at Columbia University

Peggy Charren
Founder, Action for Children's Television

Ervin S. Duggan
Commissioner, Federal Communications Commission

Eli N. Evans
President, The Charles H. Revson Foundation

Leonard Garment
Partner, Dickstein, Shapiro & Morin

Henry Geller
Communications Fellow, The Markle Foundation

EXECUTIVE SUMMARY

Public television was created in the late 1960s as an alternative to the "vast wasteland" of commercial television.[1] Over the years, much has changed. Television has become even more central to the American experience. The wasteland, to be sure, has not been reclaimed, but today's public broadcasters are being swept along by revolutionary developments. Satellites, cable, pay-per-view, niche programming, and the prospect of 500 channels are drastically altering the environment for all television.[2] For public television, embroiled in controversies over "balance" in its programming and pressured by economic necessity that has led to increased commercialization, the changing landscape raises the most basic question of all: Is there still a need for noncommercial television as we know it?

Accordingly, the Twentieth Century Fund convened a Task Force on the Future of Public Television to reexamine and possibly redefine its mission, to critique its structure and the process by which it produces programming, and to develop proposals for meeting its financial requirements and for building public confidence. The Task Force's recommendations, which emerged from meetings over an eight-month period, will provoke controversy within the public television system and in the industry as a whole. Taken together, these recommendations constitute a blueprint for change. The majority of Task Force members are convinced that only by reinventing itself can public television meet the needs of the American public in the twenty-first century.

Indeed, driven by an immense increase in the menu of programming available, the fragmentation of the overall television audience is likely to continue. In this context, the broad national values, the linkages among educational experiences, the in-depth coverage of public issues, and the common cultural experience that the best of public television can offer seem of greater value than ever. The Task Force does not believe, however, that these lofty goals are attainable without substantial revision in the existing system.

3

Among the Task Force's principal conclusions are the following:

◆ *The mission of public television should be the enrichment and strengthening of American society and culture through high-quality programming that reflects and advances our basic values.* Commercial television is driven by a concern for the marketplace that does not necessarily capture many of the values we hold dear, such as excellence, creativity, tolerance, generosity, responsibility, community, diversity, and intellectual achievement. Without public television, there would be no alternative to programs driven fundamentally by the need to sell products. While commercial television excels at reporting the news and occasionally produces works of quality and importance, its fundamental and necessary values are reflected in the fastest growing segment of the television industry: the cable shopping networks that do away with programming altogether and simply sell. The Task Force believes that alternative programming must be available that enlarges the horizons of the American people and informs them of the issues—past, present, and future—that affect their society. Public television must never assume the role of arbiter of our values, but it can serve as a medium for their expression and debate.

◆ *To fulfill its mission in an environment of intensifying competition, technological change, and economic stringency, America's system of public television needs fundamental structural change.* There are 351 public television stations in the country, many of them with overlapping signals and duplicative schedules. Programming is seriously underfunded. Of the $1.2 billion spent in the public television system in 1992, approximately 75 percent of the funds were used to cover the cost of station operations. Our conclusion is straightforward: there must be a dramatic shift in resources toward programming that can achieve the high standards of excellence needed to allow public television to compete successfully for the viewers' attention as well as public and corporate support.

◆ *Federal funding of stations' operations should be eliminated and the resources earmarked for national programs.* The appropriation for public television in Fiscal Year 1992 was $251 million, half of which was distributed to the stations as general grants. The Task Force believes that there is waste in overhead and in the needless duplication of programming. Therefore, given that federal funds come from American taxpayers, those dollars should be earmarked exclusively for national programming that will serve the nation as a whole.

◆ *Individual station operations should be supported by the communities they serve.* While recognizing that many local public television stations will be unhappy with the conclusion that federal funds should be directed toward national programming, the Task Force urges local stations to identify the needs of their communities and raise the funds necessary for their operations from within the regions they serve. They should be substantially reassured by the fact that, as all the evidence suggests, local support of stations is heavily dependent on the quality of national programming.

◆ *Federal funding should be increased to enable public television to provide a high-quality, national alternative to commercial broadcasting, provided the above recommendations are adopted.* If the above recommendations are adopted, the Task Force believes that federal funding for national programming should be increased to help public television provide the highest quality of programming for education (preschool, K–12, colleges and universities, and lifelong learning), public affairs, science, history, and the arts. The uniqueness of public television cannot be taken for granted. Many stations, in response to popular demand and in order to attract more subscriptions, schedule reruns of commercial programs like "The Lawrence Welk Show." To sustain quality programming, public television needs and deserves the wholehearted public support that we now give to public schools, libraries, and museums.

◆ *Ideally, national funding of public television should come from new nontaxpayer sources of funding such as possible spectrum auctions or spectrum usage fees.* The Task Force recognizes that it is difficult to impose any further burden on the American taxpayer at a time of budget deficits. We recommend alternative sources of funding for public television: specifically, public broadcasting should receive a share of the prospective proceeds of spectrum auctions or spectrum usage fees—proposals that are both currently under consideration in Congress.

◆ *Educational programming must be expanded and commercialization resisted.* Public television has been a pioneer in education, particularly in programming for preschool children. "Sesame Street" is an outstanding example of one of its earlier efforts. However, public television's mission in education must also contain an emphasis on lifelong learning, including job retraining and literacy, and must strive to foster an understanding of the challenges and opportunities posed by the enormous cultural diversity that characterizes American society. Public television's educational and instructional efforts must be adequately financed to ensure that they continue to provide an alternative to commercial efforts in these areas.

The problem of commercialization does not rest solely with schools that serve children commercials along with their ABCs. The Task Force is concerned about recent reports that some public television stations promote the sale of toys as "premiums" to children during on-air pledge drives.

◆ *The delivery and dissemination of instructional programming must be upgraded.* Public television makes available many worthwhile programs to public schools, colleges, and universities. However, there is major room for improvement. To remain competitive with commercial programming for schools (that may not be better but only easier to use), public television must go beyond the old technique of over-the-air broadcasting of educational materials and make greater use of video cassettes and new interactive technologies.

◆ *The selection process for the Board of the Corporation for Public Broadcasting (CPB) should be improved.* In order to ensure the quality and independence of public television, the Task Force urges that the president select a nonpartisan committee of outstanding individuals to recommend qualified candidates for vacant seats on the CPB Board.

The Task Force notes that the CPB has been charged by Congress with monitoring station programming for balance. It urges the Board of the CPB to exercise its oversight authority with an eye to balance throughout the schedule, and not within each and every individual program.

▲   ▲   ▲   ▲

A brief history of public television and the information discussed by the Task Force before reaching its conclusions are provided in the text of the Report. Specific recommendations are listed at the end of each section of the Report, and a complete set of the recommendations starts on page 47.

NOTES

1. Newton N. Minow, "The Vast Wasteland," address to the National Association of Broadcasters, Washington, D.C., May 9, 1961.

2. See Appendix, page 41, for an overview of the changes in the broadcast environment.

REPORT OF THE TASK FORCE

INTRODUCTION

Public television was created a quarter of a century ago to ensure that Americans would learn to "see America whole, in all its diversity . . . to help us look at our achievements and difficulties, at our conflicts and agreements, at our problems, and at the far reach of our possibilities." Today, public television has come a long way toward fulfilling that vision. Public television, once a scattering of 126 educational stations, now reaches into 98 percent of the nation's households; it provides a daily national program service of high caliber to its more than 350 local affiliates; and it receives and expends more than one billion dollars a year.[1]

This steady growth has been more than matched by a phenomenal growth in telecommunications that threatens public television's ability to compete for audience attention—and public support—in the future. When the Carnegie Commission on Educational Television set forth its vision of the role public television could play in 1967, there were three commercial networks offering alternative programming. Today, most American homes have a multiplicity of channels and home video available to them. And in the future, the rapid revolution taking place in telecommunications will expand the entertainment alternatives even further.

In view of the scale and pace of recent and future change, and given that the last major analysis of the state of public television was a follow-up Carnegie Report in 1979,[2] the Twentieth Century Fund decided to establish a Task Force to consider the mission of public television in the 1990s and beyond. The Task Force first met in the summer of 1992 in the immediate aftermath of the Senate debate on the Corporation for Public Broadcasting Reauthorization Act. That debate, and the media follow-up it generated, were concerned primarily with issues of objectivity and bias, especially with the question of whether federal taxpayer dollars should continue to be used to fund a

9

broadcasting organization that some critics found far too liberal in outlook. Although the Task Force was interested in these issues, the members took as their mandate finding answers to the broader questions: What should be the purpose of public television and does public television have the structure and funding necessary to carry out its purpose in a changing environment?[3]

Before turning to those questions, the Task Force set out to define "the future" in this context. Ideally, members would have liked to address the next twenty-five years, but, given the rapid pace of technological change, it became apparent that ten years was as far ahead as one could safely venture. And so the Task Force examined four aspects of public television in detail: its mission, its role as educator, its funding, and its accountability.

♦   The first aspect of public television that came under discussion was its mission, particularly the question of how to find an appropriate balance between national programming and a locally based system. In many ways, the system adopted and maintained by public television is more unusual than ever in the broadcast environment of the 1990s. Today's superstations and cable networks are premised on the idea of centralized programming and low overhead, while public television, at least in principle, remains based on the program decisions of local stations. Its budget reflects this: approximately three-quarters of all the money spent on public television, from all sources, is spent by public television's 351 local stations to defray the costs of their offices, studios, personnel, local programming, and the rescheduling of the national program service to meet local station preferences. It is an expensive way to operate—the more so because all the evidence suggests that support of stations by their communities depends heavily on the quality of national, not local, programming.

On the other hand, the local basis of the system provides an opportunity that public television can build upon in the years ahead. Local stations involve mutual obligations—the obligation of the station to serve the civic, cultural, and educational needs of the community in which it operates, and the parallel obligation of the community to support its station with funds and resources.

Public television's local stations are a disparate group with differing mandates. Yet all face common challenges, such as technological developments that make some of their traditional roles tangential or even unnecessary. For example, new methods of disseminating instructional and educational video—such as digital compression, fiber-optic wiring, and satellite capability—reduce the need for local rebroadcasting points.[4] Additionally, the increasing ability to bring ever more channels into more and more homes will make it harder for public television stations to maintain their visibility unless they are performing functions valued by the community. The Task Force believes that most stations have this capability, but it is clear that not all local stations perceive the urgency of these developments.

Public television must also find a way to meet the demand for high-quality national programming. Most of this—the prime-time feed, children's programs, and some educational programming—is provided by the stations' own organization, the Public Broadcasting Service (PBS). In the overall context of American television, PBS's national program service remains a startling contrast to most of the commercial television available. Its continuing series (from "Sesame Street" to the "MacNeil/Lehrer NewsHour," from "Nova" to "American Playhouse") sustain a level of excellence remarkable in any kind of television; and it is capable, on occasion, of extraordinary achievements like "The Civil War."

Public television's continuing ability to sustain this level of excellence in the future is in question. National programming is seriously under-funded (not more than one-quarter of public television's total revenue is spent on it). It is drawn from too narrow a segment of the nation (three public television stations account for well over half the production for the national schedule). And it is heavily dependent on corporate funding, which now pays for 30 percent of all national programming. If public television is to maintain, and hopefully increase, its impact in the 500-channel environment of the not-too-distant future, national programming must shine like a beacon—and that will require both creative and financial nourishment.

◆   The second aspect of public television examined by the Task Force was its role as educator. Unquestionably, the educational and instructional output of the system is impressive by any standard. It is one of the nation's major educational resources, and one that should be cherished and built upon in this decade. Nowhere is this more true than in the field of adult education. People are the major resource of this country: in a competitive world, we depend on our continuing access to information, education, and training for our well-being and prosperity. Television, with its enor-mous reach and economies of scale, reinforced by the development of interactive technology and computer software of all kinds, is a natural instrument of adult education, both practical and academic. Public tele-vision already has made a substantial contribution in this area, but the Task Force believes there is an urgent need to go further.

In preschool and children's programming, public television is far ahead of its peers. In K–12 instructional programming as a whole, the output is generally very impressive. But there is an important difference between the making of these programs (in which public television is preeminent) and their production and dissemination. Here, the Task Force believes, public television is in some danger of being left behind, not for lack of will, but for lack of resources. While public television is already involved with some of the new technologies, under existing financial restraints it cannot possibly keep up with the pace of change. Public television must explore new methods of production and dissemination to make its outstanding instructional programming as widely available as possible, and in as many different formats as teachers and students need.

In all of this—education, national programming, and the contribution of local stations to their own communities—the Task Force sees not only enormous opportunities but also a great need. The forces behind the coming revolutionary changes in telecommunications are commercial in origin and commercial in objective. It is therefore vital that there be a significant public and noncommercial element in the "mix"—an element driven neither by advertising nor by profit. With adequate funding and excellent leadership, public television can be as firmly established as public education as an American priority.

♦   The third aspect of public television that came under scrutiny is its funding. In total, some 46 percent of public television's revenue is provided by taxpayer dollars (16 percent from the federal government and 30 percent from local and state governments, including state colleges and universities). The Task Force believes that government support of public broadcasting is appropriate. At the state and local levels, government funding acknowledges the significant role stations play in education, public service, and local communications of all kinds—a role that should be considerably enhanced in the next few years. At the national level, federal funding, although relatively modest, is effectively the cornerstone of the entire system—the "critical mass" that attracts matching funds from other sources.

Ideally, the Task Force would like to see federal funding increased. The members also believe that appropriations made on a multiyear basis enable PBS and the stations to develop the accurate long-range planning needed for the production of programs and series. They recognize that this is not an easy step for any government, especially if, as is now the case, most of the federal funding comes from the general treasury. With this in mind, the Task Force has explored some practical possibilities for deriving public television's future federal funding from new revenues that may soon be collected by the government—for example, from a government spectrum auction or a spectrum usage fee. If Congress enacts legislation that generates income in these two areas, the Task Force strongly recommends that a part of the resulting revenues be used for the support of public television and public radio.

* The fourth aspect of the Task Force's concern was the issue of governance; in this discussion the Task Force focused on accountability out of a belief that any organization that makes use of government funds must accept, indeed welcome, public scrutiny. The principal leadership organization of public broadcasting is the Corporation for Public Broadcasting (CPB), which receives and disburses federal funding and serves as the oversight body for public television and public radio. It is responsible, among other things, for maintaining the independence of the system, both politically and commercially. For this reason, the Task Force believes it is important that the CPB Board be nonpolitical and nonpartisan.

At times in the past, the CPB has been an arena for political battles that have both distracted and harmed public television (although this has not been the case in recent years). Now is the time to honor the prescription of the original Carnegie Commission that "men and women of achievement" be chosen to serve on the Board regardless of their political affiliations. The Task Force strongly recommends this course because the members believe that public television needs and deserves the assurance that it will be better, and more permanently, insulated from ideological and political pressures than it has sometimes been.

This does not mean that the Task Force believes public television should be any less accountable. The Congress and state legislatures must continue their statutory examination of the way public funds are used, and viewers will continue to protest openly any programs they feel may be biased or lacking in objectivity. This oversight is not only customary, but also a healthy check on the use of the taxpayers' money.

Over the course of sixty years, television has evolved into a central purveyor of information to all Americans. In 1969, most adults still relied on newspapers for news and commentary, but they were also able to watch Neil Armstrong land on the Moon. In the 1990s, television has become the pervasive medium of communication; the introduction of new technologies, such as cable television, allows viewers to watch many channels, some of them dedicated to a single subject such as sports or comedy and almost all of them propelled by generating profits. In this environment, the diversity and high quality offered by public television is more important than ever before.

This is the premise on which the Task Force based its Report. Some of its recommendations call for changes within public television, particularly in the allocation of available resources. But it is not the Task Force's intention to micromanage public television. Rather, the Task Force has concentrated on making recommendations of principle, targeted to improve the only noncommercial television service available in the United States. Its recommendations are all aimed at ensuring that public television is structured and supported so that its success can be measured by the excellence of its programming, not—as commercial channels do—by the amount of its advertising revenue.

PUBLIC TELEVISION'S MISSION

The Task Force believes that the mission of public television should be the enrichment and strengthening of American society and culture through high-quality programming that reflects and advances our basic values. Inherent in that mission is its role as an alternative to commercial television, which is driven by concern for the marketplace, and therefore fails to capture many of the values we hold dear, such as excellence, creativity, tolerance, generosity, responsibility, community, diversity, concern for others, and intellectual achievement.

Although commercial television does excel at reporting the news and occasionally produces works of quality and lasting importance, its fundamental and necessary values are reflected in the fastest growing segment of the television industry: the cable shopping networks that do away with programming altogether and simply sell. The Task Force believes that the alternative programming provided by public television must serve to enlarge the horizons of the American people and inform them of the issues—past, present, and future—that affect their society. At the same time, public television must never assume the role of arbiter of our values; it should instead serve as a medium for expressing and debating them.

These principles echo the conclusions reached by the Carnegie Commission in 1967 when it attempted to set out clear guidelines for the mission, structure, and funding of public television. Dissatisfied with the uniformity and blandness of the programs available on the existing commercial system, the commission made a case for a television system that would tap the diversity of American life. As evidence of the need for such an alternative, it stated:

> America is geographically diverse, ethnically diverse, widely diverse in its interests. American society has been proud to be open and pluralistic, repeatedly enriched by the tides of immigration and the flow of social thought. Our varying regions, our varying religious and national and racial groups, our varying needs and social and intellectual interests are the fabric of the American tradition.[5]

In 1993, that observation is still valid. Public television has not yet realized the potential the first Carnegie report envisioned for a number of reasons:

- Competition for viewers' attention has expanded greatly due to the proliferation of channels offered by cable television and the growth of home video.

- Public television relies on corporate and business underwriting for almost one-third of the funding of national programming; this undercuts its noncommercial character.

- The independence of public television, particularly in public affairs programming, has been undermined by its reliance on congressional authorizations and the political nature of past appointments to the CPB Board.

- Public television's unique educational and instructional programming faces competition from less expensive and sometimes lower quality services provided by commercial video companies and textbook publishers; these providers are moving into the business of supplying schools and colleges with tailor-made video and computer software, often with advertising interrupting the programs.

- Lack of adequate funding has caused many public television stations to resort to broadcasting "mass appeal" programming in order to attract viewer contributions during on-air fundraising drives.

The quality of public television's national programming is not in doubt. Titles like "Nova," "The American Experience," "Masterpiece Theatre," "Great Performances," "Nature," "The MacNeil/Lehrer NewsHour," "Frontline," "American Playhouse," and several others, are recognized as hallmarks of excellence. So are the children's titles—"Sesame Street," "Mr. Rogers' Neighborhood," "Reading Rainbow," "Where in the World Is Carmen Sandiego?" and the recent "Ghostwriter." There have been equally distinguished major series such as "Civilization and the Jews," "The Civil War," "Eyes On The Prize," "Columbus and the Age of Discovery," and "The Prize." And public television's instructional programming includes some of the outstanding titles available to schools, such as "3–2–1 Contact," "Futures," "French in Action." To public television's credit, this is the programming that more than five million individuals think so highly of that they are prepared voluntarily to subscribe more than $280 million a year to their local stations to support them.

It is tempting to conclude that so long as the general quality of programming is high, the other problems facing public television can be ignored. Unfortunately, that is not a solution. Among other things, there simply are not enough programs and series that meet the standards of the titles mentioned above. Furthermore, all the programs cited here are national programs. And in spite of its central role in attracting individual subscribers to public television, national programming accounts for only one-quarter of public television's annual expenditure. Most of the remainder is spent locally to support 351 separate stations. How to maintain a strong national program within a locally based public television system is one of the central issues addressed by the Task Force.

NATIONAL PROGRAMMING

In his now-famous 1961 speech to the National Association of Broadcasters, Newton Minow said that, "program materials should enlarge the horizons of the viewer, provide him with wholesome entertainment, afford helpful stimulation, and remind him of the responsibilities which the citizen has toward his society." He was quoting a passage from the commercial broadcasters' Television Code. Today it is clear that commercial television is not and will not be guided by those objectives. In contrast, PBS's mission in supplying the National Program Service *should* be premised on those goals. Only by providing a high-quality alternative to commercial television does public television serve the public interest and deserve public support. This means providing programs—and an overall schedule—that are either unique or more informative than those of other broadcasters and cable channels. An obvious example is "The MacNeil/Lehrer NewsHour," which is not necessarily an alternative to the networks' evening news programs, but certainly provides commentary and in-depth analysis unavailable on any other channel.

PBS's national programming should have another objective—one much harder to achieve. It should take risks. One of the principal justifications for noncommercial broadcasting has to be its (comparative) freedom from commercial pressures and its consequent ability to avoid the bland and, where necessary, to embrace controversy.

The Task Force is fully aware of the requirements for objectivity, fairness, and balance in programming, and of the CPB's recent actions to enforce these. It notes that, while the CPB Board believes "it is generally desirable that all controversial programs be internally balanced," the Board also acknowledges that "In some cases—such as 'point of view' programs—[internal balancing] may be neither possible nor desirable. Such programs, the Board believes, should be balanced in the programming schedule over a reasonable period of time."[6] This policy is similar to that of most other public broadcasters throughout the world. The Task Force believes that nothing should impede the ability of public television to be innovative, to take risks, and to tackle interesting and controversial subjects in forceful and creative ways. The need for overall balance must not be an excuse to shun unpopular views or difficult subjects.

PBS has made significant progress in recent years in broadcasting programs that reflect the growing diversity of American society. Its sources of programming, on the other hand, appear to have narrowed. Between them, three public television stations provide about 60 percent of the national schedule. The Children's Television Workshop provides another 16 percent. The remainder is acquired from abroad or produced independently. More than 300 local stations contribute nothing. The lack of production resources is a cause for concern and a failure to honor the goals set out by the 1967 Commission:

> Public Television can open a wide door to greater expression and cultural richness for creative individuals and important audiences. It should seek out able people whose talents might otherwise not be known and shared. The search for new or unrecognized ability should include but not be limited to conventional ideas of talent. There should be a search for the unusual, for the commonplace skill uncommonly mastered, for the rare personality, for the familiar expressing itself in new ways.[7]

The Task Force believes that an important part of PBS's mission in national programming is to be more aggressive in seeking talent that can provide a broader menu of ideas and skills.

Independent producers are particularly disadvantaged by the fact that most national programming is produced by several large stations. Although independents produce nearly 20 percent of all national programming, most of this is channeled to PBS through three public television stations. Independent producers working in other areas of the country find it hard to gain access to the national schedule—partly, at any rate, because their local stations are not in the business of producing programs.

It is therefore imperative that public television (and PBS in particular) ensure that all creative, talented producers who are willing to work within public television's budget constraints have an opportunity to bid for its production funds. That includes producers in the commercial television and film industries, as well as independents and public television stations. It is the responsibility of PBS to establish and make widely known its priorities and its rationale for program development, so that all producers—commercial as well as noncommercial—are encouraged to bid for funding and informed of what is being sought for the national schedule. This would allow public television to fulfill Newton Minow's vision set forth in his 1961 speech:

> We need imagination in programming, not sterility; creativity, not imitation; experimentation, not conformity; excellence, not mediocrity. Television is filled with creative, imaginative people. You must strive to set them free.[8]

The Task Force believes that public television's criteria for the success or failure of programs must be different from those used by commercial television. Ratings are neither an adequate nor an appropriate criterion. They are relevant, yes. It is important to know who is watching, and ratings do provide useful demographic information. But there are other measurements that the Task Force considers of much greater importance to public television; these include filling gaps in overall media coverage, giving prominence to ideas or viewpoints that might not otherwise be seen or heard, providing programs for minorities and minority opinion, encouraging new talent, and courageously taking on controversial issues. When Newton Minow lamented the importance of ratings over thirty years ago, he wisely concluded that, "we all know that people would more often prefer to be entertained than stimulated or informed. But your obligations are not satisfied if you look only to popularity as a test of what to broadcast."

Above all, quality must be made the primary criterion. However many additional services and networks PBS may be running by the end of the century (and most of them will be educational in some form), the Task Force believes that PBS's national prime time and children's program feeds will remain paramount because they will always be the most visible of public television's activities. For that reason alone, the high quality of programming must be preserved at all costs.

Program promotion is also an essential element in reaching viewers. Even an excellent program will not have the impact it deserves if it is not brought to the notice of the public. Promotion is an expensive business, but the Task Force believes PBS needs to allocate more resources to it in the future than it does now.

Paradoxically, a high-quality PBS national program schedule—different from all other sources of programs—may shine more brightly in a 500-channel universe than it does in a 30- or 40-channel environment. As cable television channels proliferate, the advertising dollars available to each of them and to the networks will diminish. Without sufficient funds for original production, cable services will move toward cheaper programming. *Business Week* recently predicted that "we could end up with a 500-channel strip mall of home-shopping services and pay-per-view movies. That's certainly convenient. But we are forgetting that laughter and tears, not discount jewelry, made television worth watching in the first place."[9] If public television fulfills its true mission, it will provide much more of the "laughter and tears."

LOCAL STATIONS

The primary mission of local public television stations is service to their communities, although the nature of that mission varies from station to station. Some are big city stations licensed by community nonprofit organizations;

some are college or university stations; some are part of statewide telecommunications networks; and some are licensed to local educational or municipal authorities. Only a handful of stations have entirely distinctive missions: KBDI in Denver, KMPT in San Francisco, and WHMM in Washington, D.C., for instance, are all programmed specifically for minority audiences.

In each category, there are examples of missions accomplished. Some state networks have been notably successful in creating (and often sharing with others) outstanding educational resources: South Carolina and Kentucky are two examples. Some states are investing heavily in up-to-date public telecommunications networks linking public, educational, law enforcement, and health care institutions throughout the state: Iowa and Nebraska are two examples. Several big city stations have impressive records in national and local programming. Regional and nationwide groups of stations have achieved impressive results from collaborative projects (the fifteen urban stations who are part of the so-called Nitty Gritty City Group provide a very striking example). And a large number of stations take part in, or have created, their own outreach projects.

The 175 licensees that operate the system's 351 local stations are the sovereign bodies of public television. They hold the licenses to broadcast. PBS is not a broadcaster; it is a private nonprofit corporation whose members are these licensees. Nor is the CPB a broadcaster; it is the oversight body of public broadcasting and the organization that receives and disburses federal funding.

This decentralized structure is both a strength and a weakness for public television. For one thing, it is very expensive: the stations spend nearly three-quarters of public television's total revenues, most of it on local production and overhead, and on purchasing additional programming with which to augment and reschedule the national program feed they receive from PBS. Local programming produced by the stations is enormously variable and is generally seen by less than 1 percent of the available television audience. Noticeably less local programming is produced today than a few years ago: many stations have had to forego it entirely because of its cost.

There are no accurate figures on the number of local programs produced annually, but there are sufficient examples to demonstrate that the quantity is modest and declining. Covering their overhead (which almost always includes a studio complex), paying their PBS dues, contributing their share of the cost of national and acquired programming, and bearing the cost of fundraising campaigns is as much as many stations can manage. Without exception, they maintain maximum independence from the center, and very often have little in common with one another.

These stations, however, do face a common problem. Within the next ten years their communities will be wired for between 200 and 500 cable channels, as well as direct broadcast satellite (DBS) technology. At that stage, these local stations must either be so firmly anchored in their communities that their communities will support and nourish them, or they will cease to exist. It is this prospect that makes it essential for each public television station to define (and if necessary, redefine) its mission in its own community. And it must do so now. Moreover, the Task Force believes this should be done without making any assumptions about a station's continuing entitlement to support for its operations through federal funding. The only exceptions should be those few locations where poverty or geographic remoteness makes the maintenance of public television stations impossible without some support from federal funding.

Local stations are so varied in their purposes, roles, and locations that the Task Force is skeptical of the value of advocating any one model for stations to use when defining their missions. The stations themselves have discussed the concepts of the "electronic public library" and "electronic town square." There are undoubtedly elements within these models that may be appropriate for the majority of stations, but most important is the potential noted by the first Carnegie Commission:

> Public Television programming can deepen a sense of community in local life. It should show us our community as it really is. It should be a forum for debate and controversy. It should bring into the home meetings, now generally untelevised, where major public decisions are hammered out, and occasions where people of the community express their hopes, their protests, their enthusiasms, and their will. It should provide a voice for groups in the community that may otherwise be unheard.[10]

The Task Force agrees with this statement. Moreover, the Task Force believes that one role in particular should be of paramount importance to virtually all public stations: They should be a vital force in involving and engaging the public in local, statewide, and national civic affairs. In this regard, it is noteworthy that very few communities have yet made good use of the so-called PEG channels (the public, educational, and governmental cable channels provided for by the 1984 Cable Act). Between 80 percent and 90 percent of the capacity of these channels is still unutilized. The cable industry is rightly proud of its sponsorship of the national C-SPAN channels, but there are still very few local C-SPAN-type operations in this country, despite the obvious need for coverage of town meetings, city councils, school boards, open meetings with officials and elected representatives, and other civic activities.

The educational channels present a different, but equally worthwhile, challenge. Public television stations (through the use of their studios, equipment, and personnel) could play an important role in activating these channels for community groups, educational institutions, and cable initiatives, including continuing education. A percentage of the cable franchise fee that is levied on cable operators and currently paid *in toto* to the cities for their discretionary use should be mandated to support these essential civic, educational, and local public services.

Public television stations can anticipate much more local competition than they have been accustomed to. Commercial organizations will see advantages and potential profits in being able to communicate locally, especially in ways that new technologies will encourage. Cable companies are likely to involve themselves much more extensively in local programming. Publishing companies will become increasingly committed to the educational scene as they develop sophisticated electronic and optical methods of publishing and distributing scholastic materials. The PEG channels (whether or not they are activated by local public television stations) are attractive vehicles for both public and private community groups.

The Task Force believes that a legitimate (and perhaps the only legitimate) test of how well a local station is fulfilling its mission is whether it can be supported and financed within its local community, without recourse to federal subsidies. It is therefore concerned about the excessive number of local stations. Over one hundred of the system's 351 stations substantially overlap one another—geographically and, more seriously, often in the duplication of program schedules. The Task Force believes that, unless overlapping stations have altogether different missions, overlapping and duplication of schedules are inefficient, wasteful, and counterproductive. It is certainly possible to define more than one mission for public television in a single community, but where that is not being done it may be only federal money that enables some overlapping stations to survive, which is not a sufficient mandate.

RECOMMENDATIONS

* *The mission of public television should be the enrichment and strengthening of American society and culture through high-quality programming that reflects and advances our basic values.* In order to fulfill its mission, America's system of public television needs fundamental structural change.

* *Sources of programming should be diversified.* The Task Force has noted that more than 60 percent of national programming is produced by three large public television stations. In order to attract the nation's best creative talent, the Task Force recommends that public television widely publicize its program priorities so that all talented producers are encouraged to compete for national program funds. Public television should offer an expanded venue for the experimentation and imaginative breakthroughs that have characterized its greatest moments.

♦   *Editorial balance and objectivity are requirements, but the system should be flexible enough to require them over a period of time, rather than within every individual program.* Otherwise there is no way in which public television can be anything except bland, unexciting, undemanding, and unintelligent—all of the things it was designed not to be.

♦   *The mission of each local station must be defined within its own community, and must be supportable (in terms of funds and resources) by that community, or by institutions within it.* The only exceptions should be those few communities where poverty or geographical remoteness make additional federal support desirable and necessary.

♦   *Public service should be central to the mission of all local stations, whether they have a statewide mandate, a community orientation, or a specifically educational function.* Public access and a role in participatory democracy should be among their principal activities.

♦   *Overlapping stations must define distinctive missions.* As a general principle, overlapping stations should not duplicate schedules.

PUBLIC TELEVISION AND EDUCATION

Public television has deep roots in education. Forty years ago, long before "public television" was even thought of, noncommercial educational stations were being established. Their purpose was to harness this new and powerful means of communication to the cause of education in general, and instruction in particular.

The results have been spectacular. They owe much to the farsightedness of a group of states (notably in the South) that have committed money, effort, and imagination to building educational television into a major national resource. There is a sense, however, in which the challenge of 1953—to harness a powerful new medium to the purpose of education—must be faced all over again in 1993. The medium is the same, yet it is very different. Broadcast television has been joined by cable, video cassettes, laser discs, CD-ROMs, satellites, and interactive technologies. The student body is different, too. Having been brought up on computer games and video software, it is uninhibited by modern technology and has the expectation that technology will help it to learn (and enjoy learning). There are very few schools in the nation that are not already wired for cable; all of them will feel the impact of a 200-

to 500-channel environment by the end of the century and almost all of them will have some access to satellite and other sources of programming—video, optical, and computer-driven. To teachers in poor and inner city areas, this may sound unrealistic, but as prices fall, the 1990s are likely to bring the introduction of new technologies into even more schools.

Public television must be able to respond to these opportunities in such a way that it can continue to play a role in education. Commercial television's reluctance to contribute real educational programming for children is evident in its failure to conform to the spirit of the Children's Television Act of 1990. Ingenious, but empty, arguments have been put forward at license renewal time in an attempt to show that cartoon series like "The Jetsons" and "The Flintstones" satisfy the Act's requirement for stations to address the "educational and informational needs" of children. The Task Force notes, and applauds, the FCC's recent proposal to produce tighter guidelines for the implementation of the Children's Television Act. But this does not relieve public television of its responsibility to provide high-quality educational programming, both through the schools and outside of them.

Public television can also provide a much-needed counterweight to the continuing high levels of violence on the commercial networks' programs for children. A current study by George Gerbner finds that the number of acts of overt physical violence per hour on broadcast programs for children (particularly cartoons) have increased by almost 50 percent in the past two years (to 32 acts of violence per hour). In Gerbner's view, "We all need to act as citizens and form a Cultural Environment Movement to address such problems as TV violence much as we are beginning to address global warming, by recognizing its roots, and building a constituency for democratic participation in cultural decision-making."[11]

The use of children's television by broadcast networks and cable companies to sell products has long been derided by activists on behalf of young children, but public television is not immune to charges of over-commercialization. The Task Force notes with concern recent efforts by public television to offer children toys as "premiums" during on-air pledge drives, and recommends that such commercialization of public television's programming for children be resisted.

INSTRUCTIONAL TELEVISION

Television and the other technologies mentioned above are aids to education, not educators in and of themselves. They provide tools for teachers, but are not a substitute for classroom teaching. New technologies can bring a teacher in one location to students in another (public television's long-distance interactive satellite, SERC, is a good example), but without quality programming and effective teaching, the new technologies are meaningless.

Public television's instructional programming has been popular with teachers from the beginning because almost all of it is custom-made and curriculum-driven. Accompanied by printed teaching materials and other aids, much of it is of high quality. Programming like Jaime Escalante's math series, "Futures," or the Children's Television Workshop's science series, "3–2–1 Contact," are invaluable to many teachers. Nor is there a lack of quantity: in the summer of 1992, more than 120 new instructional series were available to schools for the first time. As a producer of instructional programming, the public television community has no peer.

Of concern, however, are the methods by which this programming will be published and distributed in the future. Today, the principal means of delivery is satellite distribution to local stations, largely through the National Instructional Television Satellite System (NISS), which is run by public television's southern regional association, the Southern Educational Communications Association (SECA), in Columbia, South Carolina. Distribution from the stations to the schools is more problematic, but most of it is still accomplished through over-the-air broadcasts. Some schools do "block recording" of programs during the night, and there are several ingenious computer aids available to help teachers locate and use the programs they want. It is estimated that some 24 million children (60 percent of the elementary and high school population) receive some part of their curriculum from television and video (not all from public television, of course). On average, most public stations broadcast 5.5 hours of instructional material every school day.

The statistics are impressive, yet they raise issues of concern. Present methods of program distribution are slowly but surely becoming outdated. If public television is to remain influential in the area of instructional programming, it cannot rely solely on its effectiveness as a producer of instructional programming. As a publisher and distributor of such programming, it already faces significant competition from the cable industry, and from video and textbook publishers. Teachers generally prefer to receive instructional programming on video, rather than over the air—ideally on video disc, which enables them quickly and accurately to locate the particular excerpt they want to show. Increasingly, those who can afford to will turn to CD-ROM, CD-I, and other computer-driven forms of software. The market for electronic media in schools is expected to grow by about 24 percent a year during the next five years. Because these technologies are so expensive, over-the-air broadcasting of instructional programs is not going to become obsolete soon, but local public television stations must plan for the day when it will no longer be the first choice of many, or even most, teachers. For some, that day has already arrived.

The Task Force therefore believes that public television should look increasingly to methods of publishing and distribution that use the new nonbroadcast technologies. This will require collaboration with commercial suppliers, including educational publishers, computer and video companies, and cable operators and networks. Some collaboration of this kind is already under way. Public television is a member of the cable industry's nonprofit organization, Cable In The Classroom, and has developed several of its own video outlets (with WGBH's Special Telecommunications Services unit in the vanguard). But available funds and resources are clearly insufficient for the transformation to happen as quickly as the Task Force believes necessary.

However these forms of distribution evolve, public television's top priority in this area should be to maintain and develop further its traditional strength—the creation and production of K–12 programming. Instructional program-ming currently accounts for only 5 percent of public television's total expenditures. In testimony during the most recent congressional debate over federal funding, public television officials noted that the development of new K–12 programming would be one of the prime beneficiaries of the increased funding authorized for 1994–96. But even this is not likely to be sufficient to sustain public television's leadership in the field.

An almost equal priority is the training of teachers to make proper use of television and other technologies in the classroom. WNET, New York, with funding from Texaco, has established a program (now expanded well beyond New York) to do just that. It is an important model in the world of instruc-tional television, and one that should be replicated as widely as possible. It is also a useful model for corporate involvement in public television outside the immediate area of program underwriting.

PRESCHOOL PROGRAMS AND CHILDCARE

Many of public television's best-known educational efforts have noth-ing to do with the schools. Public television's achievements in preschool pro-gramming (and those of the Children's Television Workshop, in particular) are justly celebrated. "Sesame Street" (designed originally as a commercial televi-sion program but never adopted by a commercial network) is just the most visible example of these achievements. Preschool programming is the respon-sibility of PBS's national program schedule, and is paid for out of the same pool of money available for prime time and all other national programming. It is an area in which public television is dominant and in which it clearly pro-vides a major public service. Its continued development is one important rea-son for the Task Force's recommendation that additional resources should be made available for national programming.

Preschool programming should pay special attention to caregivers and parents. One of preschool programming's incidental, but very important, aspects should be helping parents to be better parents. The most recent devel-opment of "Sesame Street"—the Preschool Education Program project (or PEP)—is one among several public television initiatives in the field of childcare.

Many local stations and state networks have developed their own programs. This is another area in which public television is leading the way and providing an important service.

SPECIAL EMPHASIS ON K–6 PROGRAMMING

In reviewing public television's large output of children's and educational programming, the Task Force concluded that one group—six- to eleven-year-olds—is seriously underserved. It is not enough to provide instructional programming for them through the schools. Having outgrown preschool programming, they need more programs designed especially for them as part of the regular schedule—programs with educational and informational content, but programs that entertain as well.

One of public television's priorities in addressing this group (as well as older groups) should be to sustain the campaign so successfully begun with younger children in series like "Reading Rainbow"—the campaign for reading. The exponential decline of reading among children is a danger to the future of a democratic culture like our own, which depends on the kind of education only reading can provide. Public television must play a positive role not just in teaching children to read, but in encouraging them to read more and more.

ADULT EDUCATION

Education should not be confined to the first two decades of our lives. Lifelong learning, whether formal or informal, academic or practical, should be available to every American. It can be the means not only to entering or remaining in the job market, but also a source of personal enrichment. Television—and public television, in particular—can be a significant instrument of this kind of education.

The Task Force believes that adult education and continuing education (already substantial areas of public television activity) must be considerably expanded in the next few years. PBS's existing Adult Learning Service (which is self-supporting and affiliated with more than 2,000 colleges and universities) and the more recent Adult Learning Satellite Service (which is nonbroadcast and transmits direct to more than 1,000 colleges) should be among the chief beneficiaries of the extra satellite space that will become available at the end of 1993.

Adult education takes many forms. Ideally, PBS should be able to program several different channels for people with different interests and different levels of education. At one end should be the college credit channels: in this field, the Annenberg/CPB Project has already done much pioneering on behalf of public television, particularly in the teaching of math and science. At the other end should be a literacy channel: 27 million Americans are functionally illiterate and another 35–45 million are only marginally literate. Of the many services PBS might be able to provide with its new satellite capacity, the Task Force places a priority on job retraining. This is a field in which several local stations have real expertise (WQED, Pittsburgh, and WTVS, Detroit, are good examples, as is the Wisconsin state system). It is likely to be a form of programming in which local and regional expertise will form the backbone of a national service.

There is also a need to provide the more than fifty million adult Americans who have not completed high school with basic qualifications. Very often this takes the form of the General Educational Development (GED) test. The Kentucky state network has been the pioneer in creating television programming designed to help GED students. It is another area in which expansion and further development would provide an important national service.

These are merely a few of the areas of adult education in which public television is already active and should be given the means to become much more involved. In the jungle of channels available to viewers in the not too distant future, they will stand out as increasingly important services to those who need television to help them, not just to entertain them. It is a critically important part of public television's mission.

RECOMMENDATIONS

◆   *Educational programming must be expanded.* Furthermore, public television's educational and instructional efforts must be adequately financed to ensure that they continue to provide an essential alternative to commercial efforts in these areas.

◆   *The delivery and dissemination of instructional programming must be upgraded.* To remain competitive with commercial programming for schools, public television must go beyond the old technique of over-the-air broadcast of educational materials to make greater use of video cassettes and new interactive technologies.

◆   *Commercialization of public television's educational programming must be resisted.* For example, the promotion of toys as "premiums" to children during on-air pledge drives is not an appropriate activity for public television.

◆   *Public television's preschool programming must be sustained and developed further.* This segment of programming, unique in our educational process, must remain a central feature of the national program service.

◆   *The national program service should develop new programs for six- to eleven-year-olds, a group currently underserved by public television's existing programs.*

*   *The practical training of teachers in the classroom uses of television and other technologies should be expanded nationwide.*

*   *Public television's educational programs should emphasize lifelong learning.* The expansion of adult education services should be given a high priority, particularly in plans for the use of PBS's new satellite capacity. Literacy and job retraining should be two of the principal target areas, with college credit courses and expanded GED courses not far behind.

THE FUNDING OF PUBLIC TELEVISION

Public television spends somewhere between $1.25 billion and $1.5 billion a year, which makes it difficult to compare it with the rest of the television industry. Commercial broadcasters are in an altogether different (and much bigger) business, while cable networks, as centralized, low-overhead operations, are faced with none of the costs of sustaining a nationwide system of local stations.

The central question confronting the Task Force concerned federal funding—whether it is necessary or desirable; if so, whether it is sufficient; and whether it comes from the right sources and through an appropriate process. The Task Force was also concerned about the effect of the high proportion of corporate underwriting on public television—not only the choice of programming but also the increasingly cluttered appearance of the on-screen presentation. The adjective "cluttered" can be applied as well to public television's frequent recourse to on-air fundraising, a development that is of growing concern both within and outside of public television.

The Task Force believes that public television's national and educational programming are seriously underfunded. While some redeployment of existing funding will help, public television will undoubtedly need additional funding if it is successfully to carry out its mission in the fragmented, multi-channel environment of the present and future.

FEDERAL FUNDING

Public television receives approximately $250 million a year in federal money. Most of it (about 13.5 percent of the system's total revenue) comes through the Corporation for Public Broadcasting. The remainder (about 2.5 percent of total revenue) comes from a number of ad hoc federal grants and contracts. In all, federal money accounts for about 16 percent of public television's income.

Where would public television be without it? One could subtract $250 million from the operating budget and conclude that public television would remain a billion-dollar-plus industry. But that would almost certainly not be true. Federal revenue is the "core money"—the critical mass on which many of public television's other revenue streams are predicated. Several categories of contributors—state governments, corporate underwriters, and individual sub-scribers—each give considerably more than the federal government, but they do so in the knowledge that Congress has already voted to provide a substan-tial level of support. Moreover, because production of television programs requires considerable lead time (major series are often four or five years in the making), it is equally important to these donors and subscribers that federal revenue is authorized on a multiyear basis (preferably five years ahead, as it was in 1975–78). One cannot argue that without the federal contribution public television would cease to exist (it almost certainly would not). But one can conclude that it would be a great deal less healthy, that it would make a much smaller contribution to American culture, and that it would be unable to remain one of the nation's major educational resources.

Discussions of federal funding often deteriorate quickly into ideological arguments. Those who believe that an enlightened government should use a small part of its resources to support its nation's arts, humanities, and culture are met by the reproof that the marketplace is a much better barometer of what is worth supporting and what is not. Those who believe the government has no business wasting taxpayer dollars on an industry so demonstrably prof-itable as broadcasting are confronted by the accusation that they are interest-ed only in a "lowest common denominator" society in which worth will be measured solely by money . . . and so on. These are the sorts of arguments that swirl around public television, to such a degree that some people who are philosophically in favor of federal funding wonder whether public television might not be better off without it.

The Task Force believes that federal funding of public television is not only defensible (both philosophically and practically), but that it is essen-tial—and that it should be increased. Ideological arguments about public tele-vision programs will take place whether or not those programs are partly funded by federal monies, because one of public television's essential purposes is to take on controversial subjects that the commercial sector tends to avoid.

Before it even considered whether public television needs additional funds, the Task Force examined the way in which current funds are used. It found that the National Program Service, which provides the central prime time and children's programming feeds, operates on a budget of $300 million, while most of the remaining one billion dollars in the system is used to finance local station operations.

The federal appropriation for public television in Fiscal Year 1992 was $251 million. Of this amount, $126.5 million was channeled directly to local stations in the form of Community Service Grants (CSGs). These grants, which are unrestricted in their use, have become, for all intents and purposes, an entitlement of the stations. The stations do, of course, contribute to the cost of national programming, but their aggregate contribution is considerably less than the total amount they receive in CSGs.

The Task Force believes that all of the federal money presently allocated to stations in the form of CSGs should be spent on national programming. It is not for the Task Force to say specifically how this is to be achieved, but it believes, as a matter of principle, that it should be achieved, and that the transition should be completed within no more than two to three years.

This conclusion is reinforced by the Task Force's equally strong belief that local public television stations should exist by virtue of support from their own communities, not because of federal subsidies. Only in those few cases where public television stations have important and clearly defined missions, and where poverty or geographical remoteness make local support of that mission impossible, should the CPB allocate federal funds for the direct support of a station's operation. This might apply, for instance, to stations that serve Native American reservations, or remote Eskimo communities in Alaska, where vitally needed public television stations would not survive without federal subsidy.

Implementation of this proposal (based on FY 1992 figures) would increase the national program budget by 14 percent, or approximately $42 million. This is the difference between the local stations' contribution to national programming ($84.6 million) and the aggregate of their CSGs ($126.5 million). If adopted, this proposal would be an important step in the right direction, but it is not in itself sufficient to maintain the current level of national programming, let alone expand and improve it. It is likely that the national programming budget (now $300 million when funding from corporations, foundations, co-producers, and the CPB is added in) will have to be doubled by the latter part of this decade if public television is to:

* deliver a schedule of genuinely high quality in a time of continually rising costs;

* remain effective in a programming universe that is dramatically larger and increasingly fragmented;

* ensure that corporate underwriting, which already contributes 30 percent of the national program budget, is not allowed to control program choices and attitudes;

* draw programming from a broader cross section of the nation and the industry than it does now; and

◆ begin to make use of the vastly increased space on its new satellite transponders by developing new programs for networks devoted to literacy, adult education, job retraining, and other important areas of public service.

Public broadcasting in this country (radio and television combined) costs Americans just over one dollar per person per year, compared to $18 for the Japanese, $32 for the Canadians, and $38 for the British. The Task Force is aware that a time of national deficit cutting is not the best environment in which to argue for an increase in federal funding, but it does so for two reasons: first, two very important areas of public television—education and national programming—are seriously underfunded, and second, the new administration and Congress may wish to tap altogether new sources of revenue, parts of which would be appropriate to use for the increased funding of public telecommunications. The Task Force noted that, in the past, many members of Congress have been very supportive of funding for public television. Even so, the most ardent supporters are facing other pressing domestic priorities.

NEW SOURCES OF FEDERAL FUNDING

Public broadcasting receives its federal revenue through a process of multiyear authorizations and annual appropriations by Congress. It is a cumbersome system, but as long as the source of the revenue is the general treasury, it will be impossible to change. The Task Force believes that a federal source other than (or in addition to) the general treasury is desirable, especially if it is a new source and not one that takes money from other needy areas.

It is possible, indeed likely, for instance, that the government will revise the current system of spectrum allocation by making unused commercial frequencies subject to auction (rather than giving them away free by lottery, as is now the case). Common carrier frequencies are extremely valuable and in great demand, the more so as personal communications services continue to develop and expand. (When the government opened up 2 megahertz of the spectrum recently, it is reported to have received 100,000 applications in a single day.) It has been estimated by the Commerce Department that had the cellular frequencies been sold by auction instead of given away by lottery, the auction would have generated at least $49 billion in new revenues.[12] In the event that a spectrum auction provision is passed by the Congress (such a measure was recently approved by a committee of the House of Representatives), the Task Force strongly recommends that a portion of the auction proceeds (stemming as they do from the telecommunications sector) be designated in advance for public television and public radio.

The government may also decide to enact a spectrum usage fee in return for some measure of deregulation. The argument in support of such a decision is that the government charges companies and individuals a fee to make use of (and to profit from) federally owned resources, such as forests, grazing land, and oil fields on federal property, while it gives away the hugely valuable broadcast spectrum. Various observers have suggested that, in return for the deregulation of commercial broadcasting, a modest fee should be levied on users of the spectrum. Commercial broadcasting would no longer be subject to overall public service content regulations, but rather would be given long-term leases, as in the case of cable. This, it is argued, would ease First Amendment strains and remove the asymmetric regulation of cable and over-the-air television (the viewer makes no distinction between the two). In the event that a spectrum usage fee is introduced by the government, the Task Force once again recommends that, in order to accomplish public service goals, a portion of the revenues should be used for the support of public telecommunications. (Another similar source of funds might be a surcharge on telecommunications sales transactions where part of the sales price includes the value of spectrum licenses or cable franchises.)

Whatever source of federal funds the Congress chooses to make use of to support public broadcasting in the future, the Task Force also emphasizes the importance of the additional capital grants Congress makes for the renewal of public television's satellite interconnection. The $200 million Satellite Replacement Fund approved in 1988 will enable PBS to own six powerful transponders on the Telstar 401 satellite when it is launched at the end of 1993 (each transponder is capable, through digital signal compression, of transmitting several signals simultaneously). This fund assures public television of a state-of-the-art distribution system through the year 2005. Somewhere around the turn of the century, therefore, Congress will be asked to fund a replacement scheme.

CORPORATE UNDERWRITING

In FY 1992, corporate and corporate foundation support—the largest single source of funding for national programming—reached $89.5 million, or almost 30 percent of the whole. Twenty-six separate corporations contributed $1 million or more to public television. Corporate funding is essential to the public television system, but it can make public television programming look uncomfortably like commercial programming.

Another concern is that overdependence on corporate underwriting will cause national programming to become too safe and predictable. It is no criticism of commercial corporations to note that they will almost always want to support noncontroversial and unabrasive programming. Nevertheless, there is another side to the story: General Motors was an early and generous supporter of "The Civil War" series at a time when most noncommercial and public television sources were not yet ready to support what must have appeared, on paper, to be a very risky proposition. Other examples of such corporate leadership could be cited.

The Task Force supports the continuation of corporate underwriting, provided there is strict observance and enforcement of existing guidelines. But its concern about public television's increasing reliance on this form of funding is a major element in the Task Force's conclusion that national program funding from other sources must be increased dramatically.

LOCAL STATIONS AND FUNDRAISING

It is true that public television programs are for the most part uninterrupted, but any viewer has to be aware that there is now a considerable amount of "clutter" on screen at the beginning and end of programs, between programs, and occasionally even in the middle of programs. Strict observance of PBS's own guidelines for the crediting of corporate and other underwriters will not, on its own, alleviate this problem. On-air fundraising is a major cause, but so is the intrusion into local schedules of what might charitably be called pseudo-advertising. General Support Announcements (GSAs)—paid announcements by nonprofit organizations that look and sound like advertisements—are an example.

The danger of the "begging bowl" syndrome is obvious and those who work in public television are more aware of it than anyone. On-air fundraising is a fact of life, and many public television stations have made a great success of it, raising $280 million in annual membership subscriptions at last count. But need it always be a fact of life?

Stations may argue that, deprived of their entitlement to CSGs for support of day-to-day operations, they will have to depend even more heavily on on-air fundraising (although how much more the market will bear is open to question). There is a grave danger that viewers will turn away from public television out of frustration at having so many programs interrupted by solicitations for money. Too many stations are saddled with expensive studios and equipment, primarily (sometimes exclusively) to produce auction and pledge week programs. The $280 million mentioned above is the *gross* income from these operations. No one knows what the real, *net* income is. It may be embarrassingly small.

The Task Force believes that stations must develop many more off-air methods of fundraising than they presently use. Less than 15 percent of stations have a major gift program ($1,000 or more). Even fewer seek to create endowment funds. Public television stations (the best of them, anyway) can be analogous to successful libraries and colleges. When it comes to fundraising, they must develop a sophisticated entrepreneurial approach that builds on the unique and indispensable contribution they make to their community.

Stations that have a real mission in their communities and carry it out successfully *will* attract funding. They will get it from the local governments and educational institutions they serve, from commercial companies (including cable companies) with which they collaborate, and from individual supporters and members. All these people and institutions must have a vested interest in the success of their local public television station if it is to thrive.

RECOMMENDATIONS

◆ *Federal funding of the operations of local stations should be eliminated and the resources earmarked for national programs.* The use of federal money to make Community Service Grants to local stations should be phased out within two to three years, with a very few exceptions in cases where the CPB determines that communities are too poor or too remote to support their own stations.

◆ *Individual station operations should be supported by the communities they serve.* Local stations must identify the needs of their communities and raise the funds necessary for their operations from within their region. In addition to customary on-air fundraising, stations should develop more off-air methods.

◆ *Federal funding should be increased to enable public television to provide a high-quality, national alternative to commercial broadcasting, provided the above recommendations are adopted.* Federal funding should be authorized on a multiyear basis (as much as five years in advance).

◆ *Ideally, national funding of public television should come from new nontaxpayer sources of funding such as possible spectrum auctions or spectrum usage fees.* In the event that either a spectrum auction provision or a spectrum usage fee is approved by the Congress, a portion of the proceeds should be used for the funding of public telecommunications.

◆ *Corporate underwriting of programs should continue, with strict observance of the existing PBS guidelines for the crediting of corporate contributions.* At the same time, by increasing the total amount of money available for national programming, public television should strive to reduce the percentage of the national program budget for which corporate underwriting is responsible (currently 30 percent).

THE GOVERNANCE OF PUBLIC TELEVISION

Accountability and efficiency are the yardsticks by which public television's structure, organization, and regulation should be measured. Any organization relying on federal funding must be accountable for the use of those funds. Public television is held accountable to Congress: its officials are regularly called to testify before congressional committees during hearings on annual appropriations and on reauthorization bills. In addition, there are a number of unofficial watchdogs, including the press and private or nonprofit groups representing a broad range of interests.

Currently, all stations receive substantial Community Service Grants (CSGs) from the Corporation for Public Broadcasting (CPB). This is federal money and, although there are CPB stipulations about its use, it is, in effect, discretionary money. The stations are more accountable to their local boards of directors and to the other main sources of their funding, such as state and local governments, state colleges and universities (in certain cases), foundations, and individual subscribers and donors, than they are to the CPB. The Task Force believes that local accountability should be increased by making the stations entirely reliant on local sources of funding from their own communities and state governments.

Efficiency depends in large part on the structure of an organization. The structure of public television is necessarily convoluted because the "sovereign bodies" within it are not at the center but on the periphery of the system. They are the local stations, which alone possess licenses to broadcast. They have devolved certain responsibilities (principally national programming) to the Public Broadcasting Service (PBS), which they themselves own and operate. There are therefore two central bodies: the CPB, which is the oversight body for the system and which receives and disburses federal money, and PBS. These two organizations are "the bureaucracy" that is widely (and sometimes unfairly) blamed for public television's alleged inefficiencies and inadequacies.

THE CORPORATION FOR PUBLIC BROADCASTING

The Corporation for Public Broadcasting is a private, nonprofit corporation, not a federal agency. It was established in this way so as to insulate public broadcasting from political interference. But it is difficult for the CPB to achieve this goal when the corporation itself is not properly insulated. Board members are presidential appointees. Originally, there were fifteen of them, with no more than eight drawn from the same political party. Today, membership has been reduced to ten, and will be reduced yet further, to nine, in 1997.

There have been times when the CPB's ideological infighting has done substantial harm to public broadcasting. Happily, this is not the case for the current Board, which has done much to improve the Board's reputation and to redirect the CPB's attention to areas of real concern and importance. Nevertheless, the Task Force believes public broadcasting should be given as firm a guarantee as possible that the damaging excesses of the past will not be repeated. To this end, it urges the administration and Congress to consider the possibility of appointing CPB Board members on a nonpolitical and non-partisan basis.

Specifically, the Task Force recommends that in the future the president appoint a distinguished commission from the fields of broadcasting, education, the sciences, the arts, and the humanities to recommend five outstanding candidates for each vacancy on the corporation's Board. The president would make his choice from this list or, if he is dissatisfied, ask the commission for more names. This method of appointment would guarantee a high level of leadership in public broadcasting, and would help to insulate public broadcasting more effectively from political influence without in any way lessening its accountability. It is a recommendation that can be implemented immediately by the president and codified into law later.

The Task Force's recommendation that CSGs be abolished and that the federal money now used for them be redirected automatically into national programming is not intended to lessen the CPB's role as the oversight body of public television, nor to detract from a number of other important functions performed by the corporation. The CPB must retain discretionary funds for oversight, auditing (although it may no longer need to audit 351 local stations), minority training, priority setting, and providing the Congress, the system, and the public with an annual report card on public television's performance. It should also reserve funds for emergency needs, and for assistance to areas where poverty or other considerations make supplementary federal funds desirable.

The 1992 CPB Reauthorization Act imposed a number of new requirements on the corporation. These include the need to review programs (after transmission) for objectivity and lack of balance or fairness and, if necessary, to fund additional programs out of the CPB Program Fund in order to correct any imbalance. The act also requires the CPB to solicit reaction to programming from the public. As a result, the CPB has now established a nationwide 800 number and a post office box number; it will initiate a series of CPB Board "town meetings" outside Washington, D.C.; and it will select local stations, on a rotating basis, as monitoring posts for reaction to programming.

The emphasis on objectivity, balance, and fairness has always been a concern, but Congress has now gone further than before in requiring the CPB to monitor and (where it perceives a need) fund "remedial programming."

Whether or not this function can be performed without impairing the high standards of independence, creativity, innovation, and diversity that the corporation publicly endorses will depend on the way the Board goes about its task. The Task Force is convinced that controversial programs, representing unpopular and unorthodox ideas, must have a place on public television. It is up to the CPB to ensure that unnecessary inhibitions are not placed in the way of such initiatives. The Task Force urges the Board of the CPB to exercise its oversight authority with an eye to balance throughout the schedule, and not within each and every individual program.

The Task Force's formal meetings were completed before publication of the CPB's proposal that it should take over responsibility for administering U.S. foreign broadcasting operations now run by the United States Information Agency (USIA). These include the Voice of America and Radio and TV Martí, and may also include the proposed Radio Free Asia, if it is funded. Members of the Task Force did not address the issue of whether the CPB should be involved in any discussions of the future structure and administration of these foreign broadcasting operations. However, the Task Force reiterates the critical principle that public television, and the organization charged with responsibility for its oversight, must be free and independent of government influence or control. Any compromise on this issue, however small, will undermine the foundations of public television.

Regardless of whether or not the administration of overseas broadcasting is a suitable area for inclusion in the corporation's duties, the Task Force believes it is time for the CPB's brief to be broadened to include areas of public telecommunications within the United States not covered by the term "broadcasting." The new technologies offer opportunities much wider than conventional broadcasting. They include the dissemination of data, the distribution of video and computer software, and interactive technologies of all kinds. These are not only legitimate areas for public television, but very important ones for its present and future. As a beginning, this might be an appropriate moment to change the corporation's name to the Corporation for Public Telecommunications.

THE PUBLIC BROADCASTING SERVICE

The Public Broadcasting Service is the stations' own organization. They (or their licensees) are its members and its controllers. PBS is not a producing organization. It was set up specifically to operate the interconnection and to supply and promote, on behalf of the stations, a national program service. That service is, by and large, one of distinction (although it is severely underpromoted).

The Task Force notes with approval the experiment initiated by the stations in 1989 to place primary responsibility for the national schedule in the hands of a Chief Program Executive (CPE) unit at PBS. Although its results are just beginning to be evident, the CPE model seems to be both more efficient and more flexible than the cumbersome Station Program Cooperative system it replaced. In recommending the application of more money and resources to national programming, it is neither the Task Force's business, nor its inclination, to suggest exactly how (or to whom) these additional resources should be allocated. It is clear, however, that a high-quality national program schedule cannot be produced by committee, but must have the sort of editorial direction and budgetary control that can come only from a responsible source at the center.

The marketplaces in which PBS operates, both nationally and internationally, are highly competitive. They often require long-term commitments (four or five years ahead of transmission), which PBS must be able to make on behalf of the system. Conversely, PBS must be in a position to respond immediately to breaking stories (as it did to both the Clarence Thomas hearings and the Gulf War, but as it did not, arguably, to the Los Angeles riots). The CPE model appears to be a good one for both these contingencies. Increasing its budget will clearly help, and nowhere more so than in the development of new programming.

PBS is, and must remain, the dominant force in national programming, responsible for the daily prime time and children's feeds, as well as for a large number of services to the stations. It is also one of the major forces in educational programs, particularly adult education. But the Task Force is convinced that it is healthy to have other sources of national programming available besides PBS. As noted earlier, PBS must also expand the sources on which it draws for the production of programs.

Public television is judged more than anything else by the quality and diversity of its national schedule. Such a schedule cannot be created efficiently unless it has the full support of the member stations, nor can it be properly promoted if local stations constantly reschedule it (at the very considerable expense of about $100 million annually) to suit their perceived needs and preferences. While PBS is the stations' own organization, it needs their undivided support to function efficiently.

RECOMMENDATIONS

* ***The selection process for the CPB Board should be improved.*** The Board of the CPB should be appointed on a nonpolitical and nonpartisan basis in order to increase public broadcasting's insulation from political pressures, both now and in the future. The president of the United States should select a nonpartisan committee of outstanding individuals to recommend qualified candidates for vacant seats on the Board.

- *While allocating most of its television funds automatically to national programming, the CPB should hold sufficient reserves to look after the special requirements of poor or remote areas where there is a particular need for public television, but where it cannot support itself.* The CPB must also retain sufficient funds to fulfill its two most vital roles: oversight and leadership.

- *In its efforts to promote balance in public television programming, the CPB Board should exercise its oversight authority with an eye to balance throughout the schedule, and avoid requiring balance within each and every individual program.*

- *In any discussions of the CPB's future role in the administration of overseas U.S. broadcasting operations, the prime consideration must be the CPB's complete and demonstrable independence from government.*

EPILOGUE

In 1854, ten years after the invention of the telegraph, Henry David Thoreau wrote: "We are in haste to construct a magnetic telegraph from Maine to Texas; but Maine and Texas, it may be, have nothing important to communicate." The Task Force would not have been prepared to endorse public television so strongly unless it was convinced that it *does* have something of importance to say to the nation in the years ahead.

From its beginnings in the 1920s (and contrary to the experience of all other developed countries), American broadcasting has been driven by commercial imperatives. The great importance of public television's introduction was that it was free of these pressures: it could concern itself with making programs for viewers, rather than for advertisers. Now, given the explosion of commercial outlets, it is more important than ever that the choices available to us should include a substantial, independent, noncommercial enterprise that has public service and education as its principal mandate.

In its first twenty-five years, public television has demonstrated its ability to fulfill that mandate. In its Report, the Task Force has offered a number of criticisms, as well as some essential recommendations for its future direction, but none is so important as the requirement that public television as a whole, and stations individually, should reexamine their purposes, their intentions, and their viability in the new environment of which they will be a part. Now is the defining moment. Public television stations cannot afford to be merely passive and reactive, as has sometimes been the case in the past. The nation has made an investment in them, and it has a right to know that that investment will yield rich dividends in the future. Local communities have also made investments: they, too, must know what services their local public television stations will render them as the twentieth century gives way to the twenty-first.

In 1991, on the thirtieth anniversary of his "vast wasteland" speech, Newton Minow reflected on its impact in an address at Columbia University:

> Today that 1961 speech is remembered for two words—but not the two I intended to be remembered. The words we tried to advance were "public interest." To me, the public interest meant, and still means, that we should constantly ask: What can television do for our country?—for the common good?—for the American people?[13]

These are the questions that public television must ask—now and in the decades to come.

APPENDIX

PUBLIC TELEVISION AND THE BROADCASTING ENVIRONMENT

The dramatic changes in the broadcasting environment that have character-ized the past twenty-five years will be vastly outpaced by the changes expect-ed over the next decade. Some of the major technological developments that will affect the environment within which public television operates are dis-cussed below.

The rapid growth in the number of cable channels will continue to pre-sent public television with increasing competition. The cabling of America has affected public television in several ways. On the one hand, it solved public television's reception problems in many areas of the country. On the other hand, as cable became more than just a delivery system and began to target the program niches that had previously belonged exclusively to public television, the noncommercial system became less distinctive in its output. Where it had once been one of four or five stations on the dial, public television became one of thirty or forty numbered channels. Today, many areas of the country receive seventy or eighty channels.

The principal change in the next few years will be a dramatic escalation in the number of cable channels available. Five hundred per household is already being confidently predicted. The precise number is not the issue. What matters is that public television (even with the "must carry" provisions recently made law in the 1992 Cable Television Consumer Protection and Competition Act) will find it much harder to be visible in such a crowded and noisy marketplace. For the time being, almost 35 percent of households do not subscribe to cable and of the 65 percent that are connected, it is rare for more than one television set to be on the cable. Nevertheless, while over-the-air broadcasting may never become obsolete, it will certainly become less impor-tant with every year.

41

Traditional over-the-air broadcasting and multi-channel cable will not be the only alternatives available to viewers in the years ahead. Satellite broadcasting will play an ever increasing role. Receiving dishes are already a feature of the landscape in many parts of the country: during the next few years they will become much more numerous (as well as much smaller). Direct Broadcast Satellite (DBS) is now approaching the point of full-scale commercial implementation. Hughes Communications' DirecTv, for instance, will be offering packages of sports events, concerts, and movies by the middle of 1994. DBS, like cable, will have a large pay-per-view element, and powerful companies are already becoming involved in it (Primestar, for instance, began as a joint venture of GE, Time Warner, Cox, Viacom, and Continental Cable). Public television has also staked a claim: 4 to 7 percent of DBS capacity is set aside for noncommercial use.

Much of this new technology is interactive. Two-way communication will become a feature of satellite and cable broadcasting in the 1990s—and possibly a feature of over-the-air broadcasting as well, with the introduction of interactive video and data services (IVDS), for which the Federal Communications Commission (FCC) will be authorizing experiments this year. No one yet knows how important switched systems, which give viewers access to "transactional television," will become, but they may turn out to be one of the most significant developments of all. The interactive element (in whatever form) will be important in many different areas of programming, from game shows to shopping, but it will have special applications in two areas that are integral to public television—education and public access.

The other major innovation to look forward to concerns the quality of the image we receive. High definition television (HDTV), heralded at least a decade ago, has gone through many experimental stages. The FCC is now in a position to authorize the use of digital transmission of HDTV systems (a giant step ahead of Europe and Japan) and has already approved plans to give every existing television station a separate channel for high definition transmission. But conversion to HDTV will be a very gradual, and expensive, process; it is likely to be at its peak around the end of the century.

As far as home video is concerned, it is hard to forecast what the impact of these developments will be. Pay-per-view and multiplexing (by which a cable channel like HBO can run the same movies on several different channels, all with different start times) are two practices that are not good news for video distributors relying on movies, but it is likely that the nonmovie part of the business will stay strong. Rather like audio recording in the 1980s, it is developing into new and related technologies—laser disc, CD-ROM, CD-I, 3DO (three-dimensional optics), and several others.

Another major development in telecommunications is the building of "superhighways" for all forms of information transmission in the twenty-first century. Video, voice, graphics, and data will travel across these information highways, linking homes, colleges, schools, businesses, government agencies, and public service institutions in a multidimensional network of instantaneous communication. Fiber optics and digital compression of signals are two of the most important agents of the revolution; the government, cable companies, and telephone companies (telcos) are its principal architects and builders. The speed with which these superhighways are constructed may depend heavily on government policy. Public television has a real interest in the outcome of this policy debate because access to the highways will be critically important in the future. Similarly, it has an interest in the role the telcos will, or will not, be allowed to play.

Under current legislation, the telcos are prohibited from having an ownership stake in television programming and from owning cable systems in their own service areas. But the FCC has already given its consent to Video Dialtone, which facilitates telcos using their phone lines to distribute (but not to own) video programming in their own areas. Moreover, the telcos in this decade will not be as dependent as it once seemed they would be on the expensive process of running fiber optic cable close to every home. Bellcore, their research arm, has developed a digital compression system that will allow them to use their existing copper wires for simultaneous transmission of video images and phone calls. One way or another, it is clear the telcos are going to play a significant role in the telecommunications environment of the future. Their relationship (or lack of it) with the cable industry will be as important a defining factor for this new environment as the government's policy decisions.

NOTES

1. The public television system consists of the 351 local stations, operated by 175 licensees; the Public Broadcasting Service (PBS), the stations' own organization that provides the national program service; and the Corporation for Public Broadcasting (CPB), the system's principal leadership organization that receives and disburses federal funding and oversees public television as well as public radio.

2. *A Public Trust: The Report of the Carnegie Commission on the Future of Public Broadcasting* (New York: Bantam Books, 1979).

3. The Task Force's brief was limited to television. Public radio, while sharing many of the same funding issues as television, has had to cope with rather different problems, both locally and nationally.

4. The Appendix briefly describes the growing list of technological changes in telecommunications.

5. Carnegie Commission on Educational Television, *Public Television: A Program for Action* (New York: Harper and Row, 1967).

6. Letter to Task Force staff from Richard W. Carlson, President & CEO of the Corporation for Public Broadcasting, December 9, 1992.

7. Carnegie Commission on Educational Television, *Public Television: A Program for Action.*

8. Newton N. Minow, "The Vast Wasteland," address to the National Association of Broadcasters, Washington, D.C., May 9, 1961.

9. *Business Week*, March 22, 1993.

10. Carnegie Commission on Educational Television, *Public Television: A Program for Action.*

11. George Gerbner, "Road Runner Begets Rambo," *New York Newsday*, February 26, 1993.

12. U.S. Department of Commerce, National Communications & Telecommunications Administration, "U.S. Spectrum Management Policy: An Agenda for the Future" (1991), Appendix D.

13. Newton N. Minow, "How Vast the Wasteland Now?," address given at the Gannett Foundation Media Center, Columbia University, New York City, May 9, 1991.

SUMMARY OF TASK FORCE RECOMMENDATIONS

A full list of the Task Force's recommendations in the four areas focused upon follows.

ON MISSION

• **The mission of public television should be the enrichment and strengthening of American society and culture through high-quality programming that reflects and advances our basic values.** In order to fulfill its mission, America's system of public television needs fundamental structural change.

• **Sources of programming should be diversified.** The Task Force has noted that more than 60 percent of national programming is produced by three large public television stations. In order to attract the nation's best creative talent, the Task Force recommends that public television widely publicize its program priorities so that all talented producers are encouraged to compete for national program funds. Public television should offer an expanded venue for the experimentation and imaginative breakthroughs that have characterized its greatest moments.

• **Editorial balance and objectivity are requirements, but the system should be flexible enough to require them over a period of time, rather than within every individual program.** Otherwise there is no way in which public television can be anything except bland, unexciting, undemanding, and unintelligent—all of the things it was designed not to be.

• **The mission of each local station must be defined within its own community, and must be supportable (in terms of funds and resources) by that community, or by institutions within it.** The only exceptions should be those few communities where poverty or geographical remoteness make additional federal support desirable and necessary.

◆ *Public service should be central to the mission of all local stations, whether they have a statewide mandate, a community orientation, or a specifically educational function.* Public access and a role in participatory democracy should be among their principal activities.

◆ *Overlapping stations must define distinctive missions.* As a general principle, overlapping stations should not duplicate schedules.

ON EDUCATION

◆ *Educational programming must be expanded.* Furthermore, public television's educational and instructional efforts must be adequately financed to ensure that they continue to provide an essential alternative to commercial efforts in these areas.

◆ *The delivery and dissemination of instructional programming must be upgraded.* To remain competitive with commercial programming for schools, public television must go beyond the old technique of over-the-air broadcast of educational materials to make greater use of video cassettes and new interactive technologies.

◆ *Commercialization of public television's educational programming must be resisted.* For example, the promotion of toys as "premiums" to children during on-air pledge drives is not an appropriate activity for public television.

◆ *Public television's preschool programming must be sustained and developed further.* This segment of programming, unique in our educational process, must remain a central feature of the national program service.

◆ *The national program service should develop new programs for six- to eleven-year-olds, a group currently underserved by public television's existing programs.*

◆ *The practical training of teachers in the classroom uses of television and other technologies should be expanded nationwide.*

◆ *Public television's educational programs should emphasize lifelong learning.* The expansion of adult education services should be given a high priority, particularly in plans for the use of PBS's new satellite capacity. Literacy and job retraining should be two of the principal target areas, with college credit courses and expanded GED courses not far behind.

ON FUNDING

- *Federal funding of the operations of local stations should be eliminated and the resources earmarked for national programs.* The use of federal money to make Community Service Grants to local stations should be phased out within two to three years, with a very few exceptions in cases where the CPB determines that communities are too poor or too remote to support their own stations.

- *Individual station operations should be supported by the communities they serve.* Local stations must identify the needs of their communities and raise the funds necessary for their operations from within their region. In addition to customary on-air fundraising, stations should develop more off-air methods.

- *Federal funding should be increased to enable public television to provide a high-quality, national alternative to commercial broadcasting, provided the above recommendations are adopted.* Federal funding should be authorized on a multiyear basis (as much as five years in advance).

- *Ideally, national funding of public television should come from new nontaxpayer sources of funding such as possible spectrum auctions or spectrum usage fees.* In the event that either a spectrum auction provision or a spectrum usage fee is approved by the Congress, a portion of the proceeds should be used for the funding of public telecommunications.

- *Corporate underwriting of programs should continue, with strict observance of the existing PBS guidelines for the crediting of corporate contributions.* At the same time, by increasing the total amount of money available for national programming, public television should strive to reduce the percentage of the national program budget for which corporate underwriting is responsible (currently 30 percent).

ON GOVERNANCE

- *The selection process for the CPB Board should be improved.* The Board of the the CPB should be appointed on a nonpolitical and nonpartisan basis in order to increase public broadcasting's insulation from political pressures, both now and in the future. The president of the United States should select a nonpartisan committee of outstanding individuals to recommend qualified candidates for vacant seats on the Board.

- *While allocating most of its television funds automatically to national programming, the CPB should hold sufficient reserves to look after the special requirements of poor or remote areas where there is a particular need for public television but where it cannot support itself.* The CPB must also retain sufficient funds to fulfill its two most vital roles: oversight and leadership.

- *In its efforts to promote balance in public television programming, the CPB Board should exercise its oversight authority with an eye to balance throughout the schedule, and avoid requiring balance within each and every individual program.*

- *In any discussions of the CPB's future role in the administration of overseas U.S. broadcasting operations, the prime consideration must be the CPB's complete and demonstrable independence from government.*

SUPPLEMENTAL COMMENTS
FROM TASK FORCE MEMBERS

SUPPLEMENTAL COMMENTS
FROM ERVIN S. DUGGAN

This Report of the Twentieth Century Fund Task Force makes a significant contribution, in my judgment, to the ongoing national discussion about the future of public television—and it underscores the point that public television, like public schools, public museums, and national parks, is a remarkable resource to be nurtured and encouraged, not squandered or weaned away from public support. I am, therefore, happy to support much that appears in this Report. I do find it necessary, however, to write separately about two points.

First, I have real misgivings about reconstituting public television's funding in a way that would diminish the resources of local stations. Public broadcasting has long been identified with the public interest, and one bedrock principle of broadcasting in the public interest is *localism*. In my view, the service that public stations bring to their communities should include serious attention to local needs. Diluting the amount of money that public broadcasting's funding sources provide to local stations could directly undermine the hope for improved local service. Such an undermining, in my judgment, would be most unfortunate.

Reducing funding for local stations could have another unintended consequence: it could cut the operating budgets for local stations just as those stations face some heavy capital investments. Converting the nation's broadcast television system to advanced digital technology in the next decade represents a major financial challenge, for example. Local public television stations may be deeply affected by that conversion, and strapped for the necessary capital to upgrade to digital, high-definition transmitters and equipment. The shift to

53

digital technology may present public stations with opportunities to make new use of their spectrum as well, giving them the capability, for example, to deliver supplemental texts for educational programming, second channels of closed-captioning material or other special-needs uses. The equipment to put these applications into effect will be expensive. To have any chance to make such technological leaps, the nation's public stations must remain economically strong. If their flow of federal funds is choked or diverted, how will they cope?

I understand the Report's reasons for suggesting alternative funding schemes. In the view of the Task Force's staff and many Task Force members, local public stations may hold disproportionate sway over the governance of public television—a sway exercised through the local stations' key role in both raising and deploying the funds for programming. In my opinion, however, balance-of-power problems within the realm of public television might better be addressed by tackling the governing structure itself. I am leery of choking the flow of public funding to individual licensees because public funding is lifeblood for many stations.

My second point is this: I understand and appreciate the Report's call for editorial balance across a "period" of public television's schedule rather than a microscopic focus on balance within individual programs. I am not convinced, however, that those who underwrite and produce programs for public television, both at the local and national level, should be encouraged simply to disregard the need for balance *within* specific broadcasts.

Editorial bias was one of the most serious criticisms leveled at public broadcasting during the funding disputes of 1992. Critics in Congress charged—persuasively, in my judgment—that a number of individual programs aired on public television in recent years revealed little or no effort to present varied sides of controversial issues. Some members of Congress expressed strong views about such bias; they were not mollified by arguments that public broadcasting presented balanced perspectives across the entire schedule, if not in individual programs. Those arguments about the nature of editorial balance ultimately led to a perilous debate about public television's very existence. Fortunately, the allies of the institution rescued public television's funding—but the lacerations sustained over the fairness issue have been slow to heal. If it is true that some programming broadcast over the system amounts to tendentious propaganda that violates even the most elementary standards of fair public discourse, those of us who support the system must be concerned. Rhetoric about balance "over the entire schedule" may be a way of evading the issue.

The leaders of public television, fortunately, have taken their critics seriously and have now put mechanisms in place to review the fairness issue continuously in the future. Their calculus of fairness and balance seems to include more than whether the program schedule, taken as a whole, is balanced. I think it is quite right to ask whether individual broadcasts are too one-sided and imbalanced. If we evade such questions, the whole debate over fairness in public broadcasting will erupt again, threatening the enterprise. I therefore would have preferred a more aggressive approach to the balance question, and cannot settle for the mere "balance across a period" standard accepted in the Report.

By these comments, I do not mean to place great distance between my personal views and the overall Report. I am gratified to have been a member of the Task Force, and I hope that its work proves useful in strengthening one of our nation's public resources.

SUPPLEMENTAL COMMENT
FROM ELI N. EVANS

I write this comment because I feel that a group document cannot possibly convey the passion that some of us feel about the lessons learned from the last twenty-five years of public broadcasting.

We are at a pivotal moment in the history of public broadcasting and the president and Congress have an historic opportunity to set new policies and point the system in a new direction. The new multichannel world is dawning and some entity must lead the "public interest" dimension of that revolution. Most of us on the Task Force believe that public broadcasting, properly restructured and funded, could be that leading force in every community in America, and this Report reflects that belief.

There are critical choices to be made in the next few years by the American people, which will determine the system of telecommunications for the next century. We can either have a system that enhances the values of democracy or an over-commercialized system of shopping channels, movies, and pay-for-play programming that leaves out a range of public purposes and opportunities. Each stage of broadcasting history—from radio to television and now telecommunications—has begun with stated high ideals of public interest service, only to be swamped by commercialization. Such will be the fate of the multichannel environment, just as it has been for the promise of cable television, unless steps are taken now, at the beginning, to assure that the public interest is respected and encouraged. The public interest shifts in a new communications environment. From history, we know that the marketplace will seek out mass tastes, and that profitable outlets will squeeze out the less profitable. The marketplace will be neglectful of the requirements of an informed electorate, the cultural needs of children, the potential of family education, the needs of the poor, the potential of those without literacy, the hopes of the immigrant, the aspirations of the working adult eager for skills and training. Many channels mean many opportunities to serve, and local public broadcasting entities, in partnership with cable, computer, and telephone companies, can help forge a more varied system of many public channels to meet the many diverse needs of the American people.

I have closely watched public broadcasting evolve for twenty-six years, having had a staff relationship with the report of the original Carnegie Commission on Educational Television in 1967, which conceived the name and concept of "public television." For ten years thereafter, I worked for the Carnegie Corporation as their grants officer for public broadcasting and served as a member of the second Carnegie Commission in 1979. This Task Force then represents my third policy look at the system, over almost three decades, and I believe it is time for some plain talk.

Two profound concerns accompanied the first Carnegie Commission, both of which have turned out to be prescient and unhappily valid. One was that congressional appropriations would bring a political dimension and political influence to program decisions. There were misgivings that Congress would become a major audience, enveloping decisionmakers with fear of controversy and the hesitancy to experiment, stifling risk-taking and fresh ideas by bureaucratic self-protection. The second concern was that the recommended new organization—the Corporation for Public Broadcasting (CPB)—would not be of sufficient prestige to act as buffer for the system, especially if its Board members were chosen from a political process that also would ultimately politicize the system. Independent governance and dedicated funding were at the core of the Commission's recommendations, but the Congress and the president did not have, in the Commission's words, "the faith to be free." It was understandable. All this was new, and theories of independence and the success of the BBC funding model in England gave way to the practicalities of the legislative process. Whatever mistakes were made in the initial structure and finance—unrestricted presidential appointment and annual appropriations were compromises that had to be made to get Congress to pass the first Public Broadcasting Act—we can now correct if we can learn from our quarter of a century of experience.

THE LESSONS OF HISTORY

Let me first address the issue of organizational leadership and give some historical context. In 1967, the original Carnegie Commission saw the new Corporation for Public Broadcasting as the critical leadership entity for the future. It recommended that its members should be of the highest quality, representing the best in America from the arts, sciences, and the humanities, from the academy, business, and law. It should be equal in stature, the Commission felt, to the U.S. Supreme Court. The people's broadcast entity deserved, the Commission believed, America's most visionary thinkers. The Commission urged that the CPB be quasi-governmental, obtaining substantial private support from foundations and individuals "for which it is not answerable to the government" and that its Board act as a board of trustees for "a sacred trust," selecting its own subsequent members, only half of whom would be presidential appointees.

It was even discussed, although not mentioned in the 1967 report, that the new corporation should not be located in Washington, but in New York or Los Angeles, within a creative community, so that it would not act like a government agency. While the form was enacted, none of the more fundamental recommendations survived the legislative mill, and the system today has evolved into a culture that is much more governmental and political than was originally conceived.

Earlier commissions have urged, as does this Task Force, a more careful process of appointment. But no president has yet done it. Previous presidents have wanted to control it; some have considered it an ideological creature of political importance, relegating it to power politics; some have wanted to reward big contributors or used the vacancies as plums to be traded for votes on other legislation. Of course, many good people served on the CPB Board in the last twenty-five years; however, I have talked to many of them over the years and even the best expressed feelings of disappointment and frustration because of overt White House and congressional interference and inappropriate influence.

The entire history of public broadcasting since 1967 has been shaped partially by this failure of the CPB to evolve into one of the nation's most respected institutions. The model the 1967 Commission had in mind was a board similar in stature to the Board of Governors of the BBC in England, leading a new American entity that would evolve into an institution "which must be vital and dynamic . . . of great significance in American society." The politicalization of public broadcasting by the Nixon presidency, especially, caused severe reactions. The Watergate tapes and his presidential papers are clear on this point: seize control, he advised his aides, get rid of "anti-administration" commentators, appoint loyal people to the CPB Board, and, to put teeth into his objections to an independent system, he vetoed the first public broadcasting authorization that provided advance multiyear funding. After the Nixon White House appointed eleven out of fifteen members, the CPB Board voted to discontinue all funding of public affairs programming and tried to remove all program funds from the Public Broadcasting System (PBS). The resulting deep mistrust of Washington by local stations created a climate of suspicion and acrimony that has continued for decades. The stations wanted to be protected, and they reacted by building a more forceful and aggressive PBS. The growth of community service grants (sending federal funds to each station) as an ever higher percentage of each federal appropriation was a result of shattered faith, political mistrust, and a survival mentality that fueled lobbying by the stations. They needed a nationwide base of support in every state or they risked being engulfed in political crossfire every time a U.S. senator or an angry president did not like a program.

A NEW START

It is time to begin again, to sweep away this history and create a new national entity that will lead the system into a new world. A new public telecommunications entity should be established, which might be called a National Endowment for Public Telecommunications or, as the Task Force suggests, a Corporation for Public Telecommunications. It must be visible, prestigious, elevated as a public-private partnership, entrusted with the destiny of the system, and able to take the long view beyond the collective self-interest of stations, in a world in which the outlets will not be called "stations," only channels of service. It must adapt the system to new technologies and turn its attention to the potential of computers, video-discs, and digital technology to meet the educational needs of the American people.

History gives the presidency of Bill Clinton the opportunity to reassess, break with the past, and build a new system of telecommunications, with a new definition of the public interest, drawing the best from the past, but with an eye on the horizon. At the least, as the Task Force suggests, the president can ask institutions representing cultural leadership in America to recommend names for a new board and select from this pool of nominations. Names of leaders from all fields should be available, including poets, writers, actors, composers, film-makers, directors, leaders in the arts, in new technology, and in broadcasting. Selecting some people from the world of the arts would dramatize that no matter how complex the technology, stations and systems and structures do not make programs, creative talent does. Moreover, such a board would wed the system to America's most creative thinkers. And upgrading its membership to something to which the most prominent people in America would aspire would restore trust, elevate its purpose, its vision, and thereby its capacity for accountability. Rather than gradually making a transition from the present structure, it is time to cut ties with the past and begin anew.

DEDICATED FUNDING

Hand in hand with visionary and respected leadership is the absolute requirement of independence that can only come from an assured, adequate, insulated, nonpolitical funding source. Without it, the system is fatally flawed because the last two and a half decades have plainly shown that the United States cannot escape the problems faced by government-funded broadcast organizations all over the world (including the BBC when it needed government funds and ran into the ire of the Thatcher government). Each Commission has been concerned about this question but each one has worried about offending Congress, or major broadcast interests, or not being "practical" and undermining future appropriations. Without tracing the many instances of subtle and not so subtle influences through the years, it is clear that some form of dedicated funds must be found for a system that, in the words of the second Carnegie Commission, should be "publicly funded yet quintessentially private." From a federal perspective there are already accountability safeguards in the system. Since federal funds amount to only 17 percent of the total funding, the federal government should depend on local control, local boards of trustees, multiple channels, viewer support, state and local funding, and a distinguished national board for accountability and free up federal funding so that it can be devoted to creativity, diversity, and national experimentation.

The first Carnegie Commission recommended an excise tax on television sets to be dedicated to public broadcasting, similar to the English system that finances the BBC. With the prospect of government auctions for spectrum space in the future, this Task Force Report, I believe, is wise in its recommendations. Spectrum space belongs to the American people and just as ranchers must pay a fee for grazing their cattle on public lands, so should those broadcasters and other services pay who "graze" on the public airways. Some portion of income derived from the spectrum, whether auctioned or fee-based, should be dedicated to a public use so that what is available in the American home and schools will serve an educational and cultural mission beyond the marketplace. That would allow a few channels of television, in the words of the original Carnegie Commission, to "be neither fearful nor vulgar [but] a civilized voice in a civilized community."

It should give every American a sense of the wasted potential that the United States spends one dollar per person on public broadcasting while the Japanese spend $18 per person and the British $38 per person. Additional funds will be needed, especially in a multichannel environment, that will bring the opportunity to create a range of services which must be programmed with flair and originality. Publicly funded literacy channels, children's channels, channels for high school drop-outs to earn diplomas, open universities, and other new channels of service will have to be created nationally yet be linked to local stations and nonprofit educational and cultural institutions. And every local station will have local C-SPAN type channels to cover state legislatures, city councils, and election debates. Increases in funding over the next four years, especially if some of it were earmarked for new channels of service, would yield educational dividends for generations.

THE PUBLIC INTEREST REDEFINED

Unfortunately, many people in public broadcasting view the telecommunications revolution with deep alarm, even fear. A board member of a major station recently said to me, "They will chip away our best programs. We'll be left with nothing unless we produce innovative programming." This Task Force believes most ardently that in a multichannel world, the mystical, democratic ideal we call "the public interest" will dictate a new visionary calling for public telecommunications.

The greatest contribution this Report can make, as it was for the 1967 Carnegie Commission report, is to try and redefine the public interest to give public broadcasting a new mission, a new symbolic name, a new structure and financing system, an inspired leadership, and thereby a new sense of itself.

Now is the time to set things straight and embrace the lessons of history. We cannot turn away from government funding simply because a system flawed at birth has not worked well enough. The original system recommended by the 1967 Carnegie Commission has not been tried, and there is too much of the people's work to be done. We must return to the idealism that gave public broadcasting its birthright, even as it faces the challenges that summon the best people this country has to offer to lead the system through the complex multichannel world into the twenty-first century. It is difficult to convey to the American people all the programs they do *not* see: they can only imagine the roads not taken out of fear of controversy, the ideas that never get a chance because of a risk-averse bureaucracy, the ease with which the ordinary crowds out the original. Each success story in the last twenty-five years is a saga of personal courage, often by a remarkable individual with a special vision who succeeded in spite of the politics of the system: Joan Cooney's "Sesame Street"; Abba Eban's "Heritage: Civilization and the Jews"; Robert MacNeil and Jim Lehrer's "NewsHour"; Bill Moyers' "The Power of Myth with Joseph Campbell"; Ken Burns's "The Civil War"; Henry Hampton's "Eyes on the Prize." How many other extraordinary ideas await a liberated system that rewards creativity, reaches out for the new and the untried, embraces individual and undiscovered talent, and is searching for the unique idea?

Of one thing I am sure: set the system free; give it the funds it needs; insulate it from fear of Congress; turn the future over to our wisest and most creative leaders; attract the best talent our country has to offer; provide it with multiple channels into the home; open it to the creative impulse and make common cause with the dreamers, and I am certain that the American people will be better informed, and more profoundly served, even inspired, at what such a new system might accomplish.

SUPPLEMENTAL COMMENT
FROM HENRY R. KRAVIS

In general, I believe that the Report addresses the right issues and presents them and the concluding recommendations in a persuasive and meaningful context. The Report's emphasis on education is something I wholeheartedly endorse. The mission statement is well-crafted and, while I believe many of the mission recommendations are self-evident, the Report's comments concerning the role of overlapping stations are right on the mark. Hopefully it will be vigorously pursued by the public television community.

My concerns still lie in the Report's recommendations dealing with how federal funds are to be used and the Report's continuing criticism of the programming role played by the major public television producing stations.

We are all cognizant of the fragility of public television funding at all levels, and I think there is broad agreement that more money is needed for quality national programming. However, I am very concerned that the financial well-being of local stations will be put at risk by diverting all federal funds to national program production. I am far less confident than the Task Force is that alternative funding sources can be found easily at the local level to replace this vital revenue stream. I am also deeply concerned that implicit in this proposal is the creation of a programming "superpower" to administer and dispense these national programming dollars—an outcome that would undermine and contradict the Report's own recommendations for more program diversity. I fear that the aggregation of federal dollars for national programming could lead to more programming centralization rather than less. The Report is very vague on this critical issue of fund aggregation, simply saying, "it is not for the Task Force to say specifically how this is to be achieved, but it believes, as a matter of principle, that it should be achieved."

On the subject of program diversity, I, too, support and admire the goals expressed by the Carnegie Commission and by former FCC Chairman Newton Minow as quoted in the Report. I take exception, however, to the Task Force's continuing belief that the mechanism and the resources to meet those goals are somehow missing. As far as ensuring program diversity, the mechanism is in place through PBS's Chief Program Executive (CPE) unit, which has complete flexibility in choosing its program suppliers. If the office of the Chief Program Executive is doing its job effectively, program diversity should be assured.

Additionally, by keeping some federal funds at the local level, stations have greater financial flexibility to buy programs from sources other than PBS, a further assurance of diversity. Removing these funds from station budgets will severely limit this programming independence.

As far as program resources are concerned, the three production centers cited in the Report are the ones that basically shaped the quality national programming landscape we take pride in today, and, in all likelihood, will continue to do so for many years to come. The fact that public television has these fine producing organizations within its own system is a reality that should be cherished, not diminished. These institutions worked long and hard to develop their production skills, organize their infrastructures, and nurture and build their creative talents. The fact that they are responsible for 60 percent of the national schedule is a testament to their abilities and reputations, and not the result of any unfair market forces at work. Under the aegis of PBS's Chief Program Executive unit, these production centers compete for funding as do all other program providers.

On the issue of independents, the fact that most of the national programming produced by independent producers is channeled to PBS through three major stations reflects the advantages, rather than the disadvantages, that geographically diverse independent producers receive in associating themselves with institutions that have the infrastructure (e.g., programming, technical, legal, financial, marketing) to support their projects and their specific needs.

In this context, I strongly believe that the recommendation concerning the diversification of program sources should have included language supportive of these institutions, acknowledging both their contributions and the risks they take on behalf of the system as a whole. A recommendation that provided some incentives for these institutions would have been equally appropriate.

I cannot accept the final Report as it applies to these issues without some modifications, such as: giving greater recognition to the financial risks stations will bear should all federal funds be diverted to national program production; acknowledging the importance of federal dollars at the local level in allowing for greater, not less, programming flexibility; applying some caution to the possibility that one huge pot of money for national programming might lead to the creation of an all too powerful single source of programming; balancing the concerns of the independent producing community by acknowledging the important relationship that exists between producing stations and this community as evidenced by the quality of independently produced work presented by these institutions; and recognizing the vital role of the large producing stations, which should be rewarded, rather than diminished, for their accomplishments and the risks they take.

I believe my suggestions provide a necessary and appropriate balance to the points made in the Report without, in any way, diminishing the importance of the Report's recommendations.

SUPPLEMENTAL COMMENT
FROM LLOYD N. MORRISETT

If public broadcasting is to be a major constructive social force in our society and fulfill the dreams of its creators, it needs to be adequately funded and have editorial independence. There is nothing new in this prescription. The creators of public broadcasting understood this; it was part of the first Carnegie Commission report, and has been reiterated many, many times. Today, unfortunately, both of these conditions remain unfulfilled. Public broadcasting is not adequately funded, and it does not have editorial independence. The idea that public broadcasting could receive federal funding and yet be insulated from the political process has not worked. The many good suggestions in the Task Force Report on the Future of Public Broadcasting may help "fine tune" the present structure and operations, but they will do little to remedy the fundamental problems. I believe that unless these problems are tackled directly, public broadcasting is likely to become ever more marginalized as a social institution.

Although public broadcasting does many things in addition to national programming, it is the heart of public broadcasting. It is distinctive national programming of the highest quality that best fulfills public broadcasting's goals as a constructive national social institution. The current conundrum is that with the tripartite method of financing national programming (federal support, viewer support, and corporate underwriting), no one has ultimate responsibility for adequate funding, and as long as public broadcasting is partially federally funded, it must be at least somewhat politically accountable. I believe that radical change is needed. Minor surgery may ensure the status quo but will not prevent the marginalization of public broadcasting. There seem to me to be two possible alternatives.

One alternative is for the federal government to fully fund national programming for public broadcasting; then the responsibility for adequate funding would be clear. In terms of federal expenditures, the funds are relatively insignificant. A billion dollars a year, in current dollars, devoted to national programming on public broadcasting could ensure that programs of excellence are continually produced and widely available. If full federal funding were obtained, it would undoubtedly mean that programming would concentrate in the areas of education, science, and the arts and that there would be little, if any, controversial, political content. The tradeoff would be the depoliticization of public broadcasting in return for adequate funding and limited editorial independence. So far, there is no evidence that Congress will provide the level of support that public broadcasting would need to create an abundance of excellence in its national work and, therefore, this road may well be completely impractical.

The second alternative is for public broadcasting to forgo, entirely, federal support for national programming. Public broadcasting would be forced to marshal its own resources and achieve operational efficiencies in order to survive into the future. This approach would give public broadcasting complete editorial independence, and allow it to tackle whatever subjects it deemed most important for the health of the nation. Many will see this road as being a mortal blow to national programming. Indeed, the Task Force Report asserts that federal funding, although a relatively small portion of total funding, is the glue that holds public broadcasting together. I do not accept that premise. It is much more likely that a strengthened editorial voice, increased public support, and more efficient operations would more than make up for the loss of federal dollars. If public broadcasting were to take full responsibility for the future of its own national programming, it might well turn out that a revitalized organization would create a new and healthy system of national television.

SUPPLEMENTAL COMMENT
FROM DAVID W. BURKE

Now that all the debate and consideration is done, Lloyd Morrisett has had the foresight and courage to cut to the core of public broadcasting's dilemma. Perhaps we shall never know the true corrosive effect of federal dollars on the system—the extent to which editorial freedom has been stifled; initiative has been constrained; or the failure to be a more provocative voice in our society explained away.

But two things we do know.

First, federal funds by their very nature carry with them a silent, but perverse, form of political censorship—an enormous price to pay at any level, but one of terrible leverage at only 13 to 14 percent of total public broadcasting revenues.

Second, as we enter the modern world of telecommunications, any such restraint on the ability to be different and intellectually competitive threatens the very existence of public broadcasting. And that should not be.

SUPPLEMENTAL COMMENT
FROM STEVEN RATTNER

I am nearly entirely in support of the Report of the Task Force on the Future of Public Television. However, I would like to clarify my views regarding the interplay of the PBS programming approach, the local stations, and the funding of both.

A Chief Programming Executive is almost certainly a necessity in the modern world of both increased competition for PBS and increased opportunities to expand and develop PBS's programming. However, the CPE, which models closely the approach that commercial networks have taken since their inception, carries the risk of diminishing the pluralistic approach to programming concepts that has been a hallmark of public broadcasting since its inception. In the commercial arena, ratings provide a clear beacon for navigation and an equally clear measure of success or failure. In public broadcasting, the mission and the criteria of success are both more amorphous. An important role for local stations is a key component of PBS's less single-minded approach.

At the same time, there are 351 PBS stations, compared to just over 200 affiliates for each of the major networks. That means two or even three PBS stations in some markets. While multiple stations provide some marginal diversity of viewpoints, it cannot be an appropriate use of federal funding to support duplicative stations. (Nonetheless, if a local community wants to support a second or third station, that should certainly be the community's prerogative.)

Finally, we have emphasized in our meetings the need for improvements in local programming on the part of PBS stations. As competition from cable networks increases, providing local public affairs and other programming will represent a comparative advantage for PBS.

Accordingly, I support the removal of Community Service Grants (CSGs) from duplicative stations while maintaining them for the principal station in each market, just as the three networks have traditionally provided compensation to their affiliates. Increased federal funding—another of the Task Force's recommendations—would provide PBS with the means to continue to develop its national programming schedule. Meanwhile, maintaining the financial viability of the core PBS affiliates and their ability to supplement the Chief Programming Executive must be an important component of public broadcasting's mission.

PUBLIC TELEVISION: THE BALLPARK'S CHANGING

BACKGROUND PAPER
BY RICHARD SOMERSET-WARD

THE WAY THINGS ARE

U.S. public broadcasting is nowhere near as significant a force as it ought to be and yet, internally, it is remarkably quiescent on that score. . . . [It] can do much more by way of vital programming, information and educational services that simply will not exist in American life without it. . . . But it cannot do these things if the institution itself has no internal gyroscope—no vision of what is possible, no burning fire in the belly, and no willingness to challenge the stultifying forces that surround and seduce it.

—Willard D. Rowland, Jr.[1]

In the summer of 1992, the "stultifying forces" Professor Rowland refers to were all too apparent around and within public television. For some months the atmosphere had been dominated by bad news:

- A long and acrimonious Senate debate over federal funding for 1994–96 generated bad publicity over a wide front: attacks in the press and on the Senate floor focused on allegations of bias and lack of political fairness in programming, on inflated salaries and financial "rip-offs," and on a lack of accountability in general.

- A powerful and persistent lobby proposed cutting off federal funding altogether so that public television could, in effect, be "privatized."

- A study by the Public Broadcasting Service (PBS) of funding options,[2] while adopting a determinedly optimistic tone, nevertheless effectively delivered the message that funding prospects were flat.

◆   Having delegated their considerable powers over national programming
    to a single executive at PBS, the stations were waiting anxiously to see if
    their experiment would pay off in terms of both the quality of program-
    ming and membership dollars.

◆   All of this occurred against a background of increased spending by cable
    channels, an evolution (which might become a revolution) in the require-
    ments of educational broadcasting, and the prospect of dramatic changes
    in the nature and function of delivery systems as a result of new tech-
    nologies.

The most seductive of all the "stultifying forces," perhaps, is the very fact
that federal funding through 1996 has been approved. The panic is over.

That would be true only if there was no future to look to. The fact is that
these events have graphically illustrated public television's insecurities about its
future; there are people inside and outside the system who wonder if it has one.

And yet public television is an industry spending about $1.25 billion a year.
It is firmly established in the experience and the culture of the American people. It plays a significant (in some parts of the country, an enormous) role in the
educational process at every formal level from preschool through postgraduate
studies, and at many informal levels as well. It boasts a national program service of a quality and comprehensiveness that no single alternative commercial
channel, however well intentioned, is likely to emulate. All this, and much more,
has been achieved in a brief, turbulent, twenty-five-year period. It would seem
that there is much to be proud of, and much to build on.

So there is. But planning for the future depends on there being a mission—
a definable and practicable mission that will unite and motivate the public
broadcasters themselves on the one hand, and those on whom they depend (their
audience and their funders) on the other. It has to be a mission broad enough
to comprehend 351 separate and very individual stations, which make up the
so-called public television system, yet specific enough to reassure us, the public, that those stations have a real *raison d'être*.

This is not to say that public television has not had a mission during its
first quarter of a century. Its founding fathers, amongst whom Hartford Gunn was
both prophet and apostle, had a very clear vision of what they were doing and of
how it ought to be done. Their views were largely reflected in the Report of the
First Carnegie Commission, which led to the passing of the Public Broadcasting
Act of 1967. The act, inevitably, was a flawed and compromised version of the
vision, and many of the subsequent conflicts within the system can be laid at its
door. But visions can, and should, be adjusted to changing circumstances.

At the end of the 1970s—at a time when PBS's leadership team included Newton Minow (chairman), Hartford Gunn (vice chairman), and Larry

Grossman (president)—a planning paper under Gunn's signature began with the following challenging (and prophetic) paragraph:

> Through the accelerating introduction of high-capacity cable and other technologies of program distribution, public television is gradually losing some of its special role of service to the public. Public television will no longer be the only provider of what we have come to regard as traditional staples of public television: programs of high culture, programs for children, special events programs, and, in general, programs designed for discriminating and poorly served audiences.[3]

In that same series of System Project Planning papers in 1978, Gunn foresaw technological developments as diverse as fiber optics and Direct Broadcast Satellites (DBS), and he urged public television to plan accordingly. But in the stop/start, on-again/off-again politics of public television in the 1980s there was little time for vision; survival was often a feat in itself.

Now, as it happens, is a particularly good time to be reassessing the mission of public television. The media ecology of this country has changed beyond all recognition since 1967: the context in which public television operates has altered dramatically. At the same time, we are able to see future technological developments with reasonable certainty (however uncertain their timing). The 103rd Congress contains many new faces and new ideas. Whether it chooses to take a knife to the national deficit, or to go on increasing it, is (in one sense) immaterial to public television. Either way, public television is going to have to proclaim a very commanding vision of itself and of its future if it is to maintain, let alone increase, public confidence.

"The vision thing" is an inexact science, and a dangerous one unless the limitations of the vision are carefully defined. Public television is a child of its time, the time of its formal establishment in 1967–68. That time dictated that it would be institutionalized on a solid foundation of localism—a mass of individual, locally based, autonomous, not-for-profit stations, which might loosely be united into a nationwide service or network. Local autonomy was, and remains, the birthright of every station. But suppose for a moment that public television had not been formally established in 1967, and that we were only now getting around to it. Would we do it in the same way? Probably not. It would be more in tune with the times and the technology to create it centrally—as a superstation, like Turner Broadcasting System (TBS), or as a nationwide cable network.

This is speculation, and it does not matter whether it is right or wrong because it is doubtful that the basis of public television will be changed at this stage. But it illustrates the point that the context has changed. Between 1967 and 1993 two radical inventions—cable television and the videocassette recorder—changed the broadcasting environment in which public television has to exist. And it is going to happen again. You do not need to be an industry seer to know that digital technologies, fiber optics, and interactive systems of all kinds are already on the verge of once again transforming the context in which public television exists. But this time public television will have two major advantages—time to plan; and the magnificent, ironic accident of history that public television's antediluvian, 1967-style set-up, with some *serious* rationalizations, may be well suited to this future.

Digital technology (already a given in audio, fast becoming established in video, too) and fiber optics, for which we possess all the means but not quite the political will, together represent the union of the computer and the television set. In the classroom, in the workplace, and in the home, that union prefigures an evolution in our methods of learning and working, in the ways in which we get our information and our entertainment, that will eventually—within the next twenty-five years—amount to a very radical change in the way we live our lives.

Parts of this revolution are already in place. Other parts of it—the comprehensive fiber-optic wiring of this country—will happen as soon as the Congress, the cable companies, and the telephone companies come to an accommodation. Certainly, it is the context in which public television must do its planning for the next twenty-five years. And, in theory, public television seems to be ideally placed to take maximum advantage. Its 351 local stations serve 98 percent of the households of this country and are closely geared to their own communities. The stations supply instructional and educational programming as well as outreach activities of many different kinds. And they have access to a national schedule of very high quality programming. It may be the ideal set-up for tackling the next quarter of a century. Certainly, it is a scenario for which a genuine mission can, and must, be defined.

Public television in this country was different from public television in all other countries in its genesis. Here it came after commercial television. Everywhere else, it came before. But wherever it exists, public television is a political football: there is a common experience of woes and travails—accusations of bias, demands for greater accountability, perennial battles for long-term funding. But in other countries, where it came first, public television is generally backed by a more broadly held philosophy. There is an assumption that public service has a genuine role to play in broadcasting, as it does in education and culture and heritage. The commercial marketplace came later: it was conveniently grafted on to the old assumptions, in some cases weakening them, but rarely destroying them. In the United States, public television has not had these advantages. Here the marketplace has always been king, and the very phrase *public broadcasting* is something of a contradiction in terms. The hand-to-mouth struggle for survival has left little time or inclination for philosophy, for consideration of what is meant by being *public*.

In any case, these things can be defined only in practical terms: no amount of philosophizing can supersede that requirement. Now is a good moment to undertake this task. The enemy of public television's future (to quote Professor Rowland again) is most likely to be "the continuing drift of the *status quo*." [4]

CHAPTER ONE

THE STORY SO FAR

R egular television broadcasting began in this country in 1940. It was entirely
commercial and remained so until 1953, when the first educational television (ETV) station, KUHT (University of Houston), went on the air. Public
television therefore originated in the United States as an afterthought—an
add-on to a dominant commercial system—in precisely the opposite way it had
come into being in Europe. There, in Great Britain and other countries, public television had not only been established in advance of commercial systems, but it had been designed for much more than education: it was full-scale
network television.

That noncommercial television came into being at all in the United
States was due, in large part, to the Ford Foundation. In 1951, and for more
than two decades thereafter, Ford helped to finance the development of educational (and later, public) television. By 1962 there were seventy-five ETV
stations on the air throughout the nation, and Ford, through the Educational
Radio and Television Center in Ann Arbor, Michigan (later renamed National
Educational Television [NET] and moved to New York), was financing programs to be shared by the stations. There was no interconnection: programs
were literally mailed out to the stations. Nineteen sixty-two also saw the first
real evidence of federal support for ETV—the passing of the Educational
Television Facilities Act, which authorized $32 million over five years for
the building of transmitters and studios. The Federal Communications
Commission (FCC) had already reserved more than 650 television frequencies for educational broadcasting, but the vast majority of these—80 percent—
were Ultra High Frequency (UHF) channels that were difficult, or impossible,
to receive on most television sets.

Indisputably, noncommercial television had been established in an educational context. For this reason, state and local governments were its most
substantial financial supporters. The majority of those seventy-five ETV stations in existence in 1962 were licensed to educational institutions. But
there was also evidence of growing community support: in 1954 WQED,
Pittsburgh, had become the first noncommercial station to be licensed by a
community nonprofit organization, and many big cities followed suit. As
early as 1955 KQED in San Francisco became the first community station to
use an on-air auction to raise funds—a sign of things to come.

Throughout the 1960s the Ford Foundation continued its support in
imaginative and innovative ways. NET in New York was supplying ETV stations with about five hours of cultural and public affairs programming each
week, and a further two and a half hours of children's programming. In 1964
Ford's annual contribution had reached $7.6 million, and there were now 101
ETV stations to make use of the programming. Two years later, in another
initiative, the Ford Foundation established the Public Television Laboratory
in New York to supply stations with prestigious Sunday-night programming.
Despite Ford's grant of $10 million (which included the cost of intercon-
necting the stations each Sunday evening), it failed after only two years—
leaving commercial networks to "borrow" formats that eventually became
"60 Minutes" and "First Tuesday."

By the mid-1960s it was clear that ETV was an industry with potential.
The National Association of Educational Broadcasters recommended the
creation of a presidential commission to study the needs of this evolving
industry. The Johnson administration, however, preferred a nongovernmental
study, and in 1965 the Carnegie Corporation established its Commission on
Educational Television (later called Carnegie I) under the chairmanship of
James Killian of the Massachusetts Institute of Technology.

At the time of the Carnegie deliberations in 1965–66 there were 126
ETV stations on the air. There were no central institutions other than infor-
mal ones like NET and some regional associations of ETV stations (the Eastern
Educational Network, for instance, had been put together in 1960 by Hartford
Gunn, then the manager of Boston's WGBH). The total income of ETV sta-
tions in fiscal year 1965–66 was $58.3 million; see Table 1.1 for the makeup.

In January 1967 the Carnegie commission published its findings.[1] It coined
the name "public television." It confirmed the philosophy of localism as being
paramount throughout the system. It recommended a manufacturers' excise tax
on television sets (initially 2 percent, rising to 5 percent) to raise $40 million,
and eventually $100 million, a year. It invented the concept of a nongovernmental
private corporation called the Corporation for Public Television, which would
receive the excise tax income from the Treasury and use it for the following:

TABLE 1.1
SOURCES OF INCOME FOR EDUCATIONAL TELEVISION STATIONS
FISCAL YEAR 1965–66 (MILLIONS)

Local and state governments	$ 26.8
State universities	6.5
Federal government	6.8
Foundations (mainly Ford)	8.4
Corporate underwriting of programs	1.1
Gifts from business and industry	2.1
Subscribers/membership	3.2
Other	3.4
Total	58.3

Source: *Public Television: A Program for Action—The Report and Recommendations of the Carnegie Commission on Educational Television* (New York: Harper & Row, 1967) p. 243, Table 5.

◆ To operate a national network that would interconnect ETV stations

◆ To support the production of programming through two national production centers

◆ To help finance productions for greater-than-local use

◆ To support local broadcasting

The Carnegie commission estimated that "other costs to the system such as the capital and basic operating costs of the local stations" might eventually raise the total annual costs of the system as high as $270 million. These further costs would be met by the Department of Health, Education, and Welfare (HEW), and by foundations and other private sources.[2]

In November 1967, President Lyndon Johnson signed the Public Broadcasting Act. It included public radio as well as television within its remit, so it had a broader scope than the Carnegie commission's considerations. In essence, it accepted the basic intent of the Carnegie proposals, but it altered them in significant ways:

◆   It accepted the idea of a Corporation for Public Broadcasting (CPB), but instead of a twelve-person board (six appointed by the president, six selected by the board itself) the act set up a fifteen-person board, all of them appointed by the president and confirmed by the Senate, and not more than eight of them to be members of the same political party.

◆   The idea of an excise tax on television sets was deemed by the Congress to be impracticable: instead, the act provided for the CPB to receive annual appropriations from Congress, just like federal agencies. The White House, meanwhile, promised it would develop other plans for long-term, politically insulated funding.

◆   The act prohibited the CPB from operating the interconnection on the grounds that if the CPB had the power not only to finance programs but to advertise them and have them simultaneously broadcast by stations as well, it would, in effect, become a "fourth network."

◆   The Carnegie commission had proposed that station operating funds should be provided by HEW, while the corporation concentrated its resources on the funding of programs and the provision of the interconnection. Congress found it inappropriate for a government agency like HEW to provide station operating funds. Instead, the act proposed to "insulate" stations from government pressures by having the CPB provide these funds. HEW's role would be confined to making grants for facilities.

The Public Broadcasting Act of 1967 established the pattern of public television as we know it. It formalized the commitment of the federal government to supplement funding from state, local, and private sources. It paid lip service (at least) to the requirement that public broadcasting should be insulated from government interference in programming. And it recognized the importance of having an independent, noncommercial broadcasting system as a national institution. It has to be said that it also legislated into existence most of the tensions that would give rise to conflict and argument within and about the system during the next twenty-five years.

Whether it was explicit or implicit, the central issue in many of these conflicts would be objectivity and fairness in programs. The Public Broadcasting Act had specifically required the CPB to ensure that public television programs "will be made available to public telecommunications entities with strict adherence to objectivity and balance in all programs or series of programs of a controversial nature." This requirement was addressed to the CPB, not to the stations. All stations, whether they are commercial or noncommercial, are governed by FCC regulations (including the Fairness Doctrine until it was placed in virtual suspension in the 1980s). But on objectivity and balance, the Public Broadcasting Act placed this *additional* responsibility on the CPB. It was confirmed in 1975 by the District of Columbia Circuit Court. In the 1975 case *Accuracy in Media, Inc.* v. FCC it ruled that the FCC had no jurisdiction over public broadcasting in matters of editorial balance and fairness, and that these were the responsibility of the CPB, which was answerable to the Congress. In other words, Congress would hold the CPB (one of public television's principal source of funds) accountable for political and editorial balance—on the basic democratic principle that if an entity receives tax revenues it must be accountable to the representatives of the taxpayers.

The immediate result of the Public Broadcasting Act was a dramatic and spectacular growth in public broadcasting. In five years the number of stations almost doubled, from 126 to 233; in the twenty years thereafter it has risen to 351.

Equally spectacular was the effect on programming. The Carnegie commission's distinction between instructional television (programs directed at students in the classroom) and public television (programs directed at the general community) remained valid, but it was the public television programming that attracted attention and audiences. "The Forsyte Saga" and "Civilisation" were first broadcast in 1970. "Masterpiece Theatre" came into existence in 1971. In two years, between 1970 and 1972, the prime-time audience for public television rose by 30 percent. Research by the A. C. Nielsen Company in the fall of 1972 showed that 36.1 percent of American households were watching public television at some stage during an eight-week period.

The program that really put public television on the map, however, was a distinctively educational program: "Sesame Street." With a good deal of help from the Carnegie Corporation, the Children's Television Workshop (CTW) came into existence in 1968 as an independent production house. The following year, with funding from a consortium of foundations and the federal government, CTW put "Sesame Street" on the air—a program designed to teach cognitive skills to preschool children, but produced with a flair and expertise that commercial television might envy. In 1971 CTW followed up with "The Electric Company," a series designed to teach reading skills to primary-grade children. It was the great good fortune of public television that CTW was there at the outset, its wonders to perform.

The success of "Sesame Street" and "The Electric Company" also served to dramatize a major problem inherent in the system. Whereas in 1964 56 percent of all instructional programs had been produced locally, by 1976 that proportion had dropped to 20 percent. In very large part this was due to the expense and professionalism required to produce programs of the standard established by CTW.

The problem was not peculiar to children's programming. It would come to a head in June 1972, when President Richard Nixon vetoed a two-year $155 million authorization for the CPB on the grounds that public broadcasting was deserting the concept of localism. A year earlier the director of the White House Office of Telecommunications Policy, Clay Whitehead, had used a National Association of Educational Broadcasters (NAEB) platform to accuse public broadcasters of trying to create "a fourth network" and of deserting "the bedrock of localism." In the wake of the veto a White House speechwriter, Patrick Buchanan, went on a talk show and laid bare the issue:

> I had a hand in drafting the veto message. And if you look at the public television, you will find you've got Sander Vanocur and Robert MacNeil, the first of whom, Sander Vanocur, is a notorious Kennedy sycophant, and Robert MacNeil, who is anti-Administration. You have the Elizabeth Drew show on, which is, she personally, is definitely not pro-Administration. I would say anti-Administration. "Washington Week in Review" is unbalanced against us, you have "Black Journal" which is unbalanced against us . . . you have Bill Moyers, which is unbalanced against the Administration. And then for a fig leaf they throw in William F. Buckley's program. . . .[3]

The issue was bias. The "cause" was localism. But the underlying problem lay in the structure and organization of public television, and was emphasized by the very considerable success of public television in those first five years.

The Corporation for Public Broadcasting had been formed in 1968. It received its first federal appropriation ($5 million), and it opened for business by giving its first program grant (to "Black Journal," still on the air today as "Tony Brown's Journal"). The CPB also made its first grants to public television stations ($10,000 per station across the board).

One of the CPB's first tasks was to comply with the Public Broadcasting Act's prohibition of the CPB itself operating the interconnection. A study group made up of the CPB, the Ford Foundation, and station managers came up with the strategy of establishing a private organization, the Public Broadcasting Service (PBS), to operate the interconnection. PBS was a membership organization consisting of all public television stations. It was controlled by a board consisting of station managers, together with representatives of the CPB, NET, and the public. The CPB retained its absolute authority to decide which programs should receive federal funds, but—inevitably—from the moment PBS started sending out programs to stations in the fall of 1970, PBS (as the stations' representative) became involved not just in the distribution of programs, but in the planning and funding of them as well.

One of the reasons for PBS's early involvement in editorial matters was the requirement of its owners (the stations) that it intervene in the battle some of them were having with program suppliers. In particular, some of the stations were uncomfortable with programs produced by two important production centers—NET and the National Public Affairs Center for Television (NPACT).

NET continued to be the Ford Foundation's major contribution to public television. In 1971 NET was merged into Channel 13, New York's public television station, to become WNET, taking with it the responsibilities and funding of NET. Its programs were often hard-hitting and frequently controversial. In 1971 alone, "Banks and the Poor" (which listed 133 legislators and government officials with banking connections), "The Great American Dream Machine," and "The Politics of Woody Allen" set off major conflicts with the stations. PBS was required by the stations to intervene. It developed a code of programming standards and practices; it began monitoring all national programming on behalf of the stations; and it was accused by WNET of attempting censorship.

NPACT was established by the Ford Foundation and the CPB in 1971 and attached to the Washington station, WETA. It produced "Washington Week in Review" and "Thirty Minutes With," as well as documentaries and election coverage. Several stations made it clear they considered its programs ultraliberal and dominated by the thinking of the Ford Foundation. PBS was again asked to intervene.

These internal conflicts, together with the dramatic impact of the Nixon veto in June 1972, shook the infant system to its roots. The CPB, lacking both nonpolitical and visionary leadership, panicked. Some of its senior staff resigned. Nixon had now appointed eleven of the fifteen board members. And the CPB board moved to annihilate the powers of PBS. It discontinued funding for all public affairs programs other than "Black Journal" and it rescinded its funding commitment to NPACT. The CPB also took back from PBS

> the decision-making process, and ultimate responsibility for decisions, on program production support or acquisition [and] the pre-broadcast acceptance and post-broadcast review of programs to determine strict adherence to objectivity and balance in all programs of a controversial nature.[4]

PBS fought back. It reorganized itself under the chairmanship of Ralph Rogers of KERA, Dallas, and was ultimately able to come to terms with the CPB because of Rogers's successful negotiation with the CPB's chairman, Thomas Curtis (but not before the CPB board had initially rejected the package, causing Curtis to resign and to make a fiery statement accusing the White House of having tampered with board members in order to influence the vote). Curtis was succeeded by James Killian, former chairman of the Carnegie commission, and he and Rogers quickly signed the partnership agreement that would be the basis of the public broadcasting system, through storm and tempest, for the next several years. It remained a fragile structure, but it satisfied both Congress and the White House and enabled successive authorization bills to be enacted into law.

In essence, the partnership agreement said that the CPB, while retaining its ultimate statutory responsibility for public broadcasting, would back off its attempt to supervise programming directly. The agreement also stipulated that the CPB would (by 1977) allocate 50 percent of all its funds to the stations as Community Service Grants (thus enabling President Nixon to proclaim the triumph of localism and to sign a new authorization bill for $110 million over two years). PBS would continue to operate the interconnection on behalf of its member stations, and the CPB would continue to pay for it. Because most of its program money would now go directly to the stations as Community Service Grants, the CPB would have fewer discretionary dollars to spend on programming of its own devising. There was to be consultation between CPB and PBS programming staffs about program funding, but, in truth, this provision of the partnership agreement was so woolly that no one properly understood it and it would continue to be a source of tension and misunderstanding between the two bodies.

Nevertheless, the partnership agreement was a landmark in the development of public broadcasting. In its immediate aftermath, Hartford Gunn, who was now president of PBS, devised a new method for the stations (now enriched by their much larger Community Service Grants from the CPB), to pool their funds and to select and commission national programs without the CPB playing a part in the decision-making process. What Gunn devised was the Station Program Cooperative (SPC). Established in 1974, the SPC was run by PBS on behalf of its member stations, and financed principally by the stations themselves. It received additional contributions from the CPB—$4.1 million in 1974—and, at first, from the Ford Foundation. The SPC's creation meant that most of the public affairs programs previously funded, or partly funded, by the Ford Foundation would now be funded through the stations' own decision-making body. The SPC system would survive until 1991.

There is no greater irony in the history of public television than the way in which this formative experience, set off by the Nixon veto, came to its climax in 1974. The PBS network's gavel-to-gavel coverage of the Senate Watergate hearings was transmitted day after day, right across the evening prime-time period—something that no commercial network could afford to do. In the words of the second Carnegie commission report (1978): "To many close observers, this coverage redeemed the system and brought it new audiences, as well as new respect."[5]

The immediate achievement of the partnership agreement was the resumption of federal funding—followed in 1975 by something even more important: the creation of multiyear funding. The bill President Gerald Ford signed that year authorized funding for a five-year period, and Congress empowered itself to appropriate funds to the CPB three years in advance. Here, at last, was the realization of the promise made by the Johnson administration at the time of the signing of the Public Broadcasting Act of 1967—the mechanism whereby public television might hope to be insulated from the pressures of day-to-day politics. Moreover, the amount of federal funding was significantly increased. The overall appropriation to the CPB was to be based on a "matching" formula of $1.00 of federal money for every $2.50 of nonfederal money the system managed to bring in (changed to a simple 1:2 ratio in 1978).

Ten years after the formal creation of public broadcasting, the annual appropriation was $119 million (compared to $5 million in 1968) and the total amount of money being spent by public broadcasting was approximately $420 million a year. Congress, taking its cue from the CPB/PBS partnership agreement, ordered that half the annual appropriation should go automatically to the individual stations. In this way "the bedrock of localism" was confirmed. The size of the appropriation was largely dependent on the stations' success in raising other funds, and the stations, independently of the CPB, were able to use a substantial part of their automatic share of federal funds to "fuel" the SPC. Many of the internal conflicts from now on would center on the stations' annoyance with some of the program-funding decisions still being made by the CPB (the decision to cofinance the British Broadcasting Corporation's [BBC] Shakespeare Project in 1976 was a prime example), and with the CPB's use of money for nonprogramming activities.

The Ford Foundation was phasing out its longtime support of public broadcasting. It finally came to an end in 1977, by which time the foundation had contributed almost $300 million to the endeavor. Its last major initiative, in 1974, was the establishment of the Station Independence Program (SIP), which, like the SPC, would be a long-standing cornerstone of the public television system. The purpose of the SIP was to assist stations in encouraging nonfederal support through contributions and greater viewer awareness. Between 1974 and 1977, with the help of matching grants from the Ford Foundation, the SIP helped to increase annual viewer support from $24 million to $58 million (approximately 13.5 percent of total funding). Today, fifteen years later, with the SIP still in operation, viewer support amounts to over $280 million a year (24 percent of total revenues).

Crucially important though that 13.5 percent was in 1978, it was dwarfed by the contributions of federal, state, and local governments (including state universities), which together accounted for 65 percent of the total income available to public television. Much of this was spent on overhead and administrative costs, for there were now 280 stations in the system. But the most visible part of public television's activity—and the part that inevitably attracted the most critical attention—was the national programming schedule, distributed nationwide by PBS through a magnificent new satellite interconnection, inaugurated in 1977 and paid for by CPB funds ($40 million): it was the first comprehensive satellite delivery system in American broadcasting.

National programming (including promotion) in 1977–78 cost the system a little less than $70 million—only about 16 percent of public television's total income. Of this amount, almost one-quarter came from corporate underwriting. It did not seem like a lot of money—it was only $14.5 million—but the major part of it came from oil companies (led by Mobil, Exxon, and Texaco), which together accounted for 12.5 percent of all the money spent on national programming. In terms of hours, they funded, or partly funded, 17.5 percent of the national schedule. Despite rigorous application of PBS's guidelines for corporate underwriting, there were accusations of commercialization from several quarters, and within public television there was disquiet at the way in which Mobil and Exxon, in particular, were alleged themselves to have selected programming for the series they underwrote ("Masterpiece Theatre" and "Great Performances," respectively).

◆ ◆ ◆ ◆

It could plausibly be argued that 1979–80 was the "High Noon" of public television. It could equally be argued that the public broadcasting system in this country was fundamentally flawed and in need of drastic overhaul (which is precisely what the second Carnegie commission was in the process of arguing at that very moment). Nevertheless, when you look at the twenty-five year period following Carnegie I, 1979–80 stands out:

◆   Terrestrial broadcasting was still paramount: cable television networks had not yet addressed themselves to public television's exclusive field.

◆   The system of authorizations and appropriations seemed to be securely in place.

◆   A "matching" formula of one federal dollar for every two nonfederal dollars was statutorily recognized.

◆   The splendid new satellite interconnection was funded, built, and working.

◆   Every state of the Union except Montana (zero) and Wyoming (5 percent) boasted public television coverage of at least 50 percent of its population (most states had 75 percent to 95 percent coverage).

+ Cumulative ratings showed that public television was viewed at least once a month by 63.2 percent of all households with television, and at least once a week by 33 percent.

+ PBS's national programming—from "The Adams Chronicles" to "Visions," from "The MacNeil/Lehrer Report" to "Sesame Street," from "Dance in America" to "Masterpiece Theatre"—was widely acclaimed for its high quality. It was also acknowledged that the "mix" of programming on the public system was unique in American television.

+ The educational/instructional side of public television was continuing to expand. Some fifteen states (most notably Kentucky, Maryland, Nebraska, South Carolina, and Mississippi) were leading the way. Mississippi, for instance, was broadcasting about one hundred hours a week of educational programming, of which forty hours were instructional programs mainly for primary-grade children. Adult education was also becoming important, with South Carolina in the vanguard (as it was in almost all aspects of educational telecommunications). Community colleges (in southern California, for instance) and community associations (like WAMI in the Northwest) were using public television for instructional courses from medical education to consumer law. Educational institutions all over the country were using series like "The Adams Chronicles" and "The Ascent of Man" as the basis for credit courses.

This was the background to the report of the Carnegie Commission on the Future of Public Broadcasting (Carnegie II), published in January 1979. During the commission's deliberations President Jimmy Carter had signed the Public Telecommunications Financing Act of 1978—a generous piece of legislation in some respects because it raised the ceiling of federal funding and at the same time improved the "matching" formula to 1:2. Ominously, however, it reduced the authorization period from five years to three years and, in effect, reduced the appropriation period from three years to two.

Carnegie II's report was a remarkably thorough and very ambitious document. Yet it was largely ignored and had almost no effect on the future of public broadcasting. It found "public broadcasting's financial, organizational and creative structure fundamentally flawed." It recommended[6]:

+ The replacement of the CPB by a Public Telecommunications Trust, governed by nine presidentially appointed trustees who would serve nine-year terms. The president would select the trustees from a list submitted to him by a panel chaired by the Librarian of Congress and made up of distinguished persons "drawn from governmental institutions devoted to the arts, the sciences, the humanities, and the preservation of our heritage," plus two representatives of public broadcasting.

• The creation of a Program Services Endowment as "a highly insulated, semi-autonomous division" of the Trust—its sole objective to be "the support of creative excellence" by the underwriting of a broad range of programs and program services. The Endowment would have a fifteen-member Board (including at least three public broadcasters), the members to be appointed by the trustees of the Trust from a list of candidates submitted by the board of the Endowment. "There must be at least one place in the system offering to artists and journalists the principal prerequisite for creative achievement, the freedom to take risks."

• "The provision of substantially greater funding than the system now receives." By 1985, the report said, public radio and television should be spending $1.2 billion annually, of which half should come from the federal government. "We recommend general revenues as the principal source of federal funds. . . . We recommend the establishment of a fee on licensed users of the spectrum, with the income from this fee used to offset in part the increased requirement for general tax revenues."

• In order to ensure that the local stations used the bulk of their new resources on programming (local, regional, and national), Community Service Grants should be renamed Program Service Grants—which might, in turn, be supplemented by the Endowment.

The Carnegie II report also made somewhat more nebulous recommendations on technology ("It is essential for public broadcasting to have both the money and the flexibility necessary to enable it to chart its own course as it responds to the future"), on education and learning (for which the Program Services Endowment should have responsibility at the center to contribute to the efforts of local stations), and on public accountability (increased public participation, equal employment opportunities, access for minorities, financial disclosure, community ascertainment, public involvement in station governance, and so on).

Looking back on Carnegie II from the perspective of 1992, Professor Willard D. Rowland, Dean of the School of Journalism and Mass Communications at the University of Colorado, summed it up like this:

> For all its passionate interest in promoting a significant advancement of what it called a "public trust," Carnegie II was too aloof from both the general U.S. telecommunications policy environment and

the realities of the structural changes and power relationships within public broadcasting that had emerged since Carnegie I to be effective in the applied political realm where its recommendations would have to be enacted. There were none of the prior understandings with Congress and the White House that had guaranteed those aspects of success achieved by Carnegie I.[7]

◆ ◆ ◆ ◆

Through all the conflicts, the pre-1980 history of public television had been a story of dramatic growth. The post-1980 history has also seen considerable growth, but a longer perspective will almost certainly show that the most important developments of this period took place outside and around public television rather than within it.

Between 1980 and 1992 the ecology of American television changed with startling rapidity. Two developments in particular—cable television and home video—revolutionized viewing habits and altered, for all time, the context in which public television had been created. Public television's response (or lack of it) to these developments has become the crucial measure of the system's health and prospects.

It was hardly surprising that public television failed to respond quickly to the challenge from cable television. To begin with, it looked as if there would be no real challenge. The most likely contender was CBS Cable, but it was closed down within two years for lack of adequate advertising revenues. Similar experiments by RCA (the Entertainment Channel) and Hearst and ABC Video Enterprises (ARTS) fared little better until they merged in 1984 to form the Arts & Entertainment Network (A&E). Although A&E did not finally get into the black until 1990, it seemed to have become a permanent presence by the late 1980s. It had contractual arrangements with the BBC (which inevitably raised the price of BBC programs to public television) and a program brief covering many areas previously thought of as public television's domain. A&E did not look much like public television. Its programs were frequently interrupted by commercials. Nevertheless, it increased its coverage of the nation to 57 percent of households by 1992, making it easier for opponents of public television to argue that A&E was an alternative—and a self-financing one at that.

On its own, A&E was hardly a credible alternative, but when other cable channels were added—the Disney Channel and Nickelodeon (children's programs), the Discovery Channel and the Learning Channel (documentaries), CNN and C-SPAN (news and public affairs), and Bravo (cultural programs)—the argument became more substantial. Opponents of public television's federal funding could argue that, when taken together, these cable channels provided viewers with the same kind of programming as public television, and at no cost to the taxpayer.

By the late 1980s there were also "alternatives" on the educational and instructional fronts. Whittle Communications's Channel One (with advertisements) and CNN (without) were providing schools with daily news programs by satellite; Cable in the Classroom had been established in Washington as an umbrella organization for twenty different cable channels, all of them involved in delivering commercial-free programs to schools; and Jones Intercable's Mind Extension University was providing degree-course programming for cable viewers.

Cable has been a mixed blessing to public television. It has brought competition—and raised prices in the process. But it has also enabled a lot of public television stations, previously condemned to broadcast on hard-to-receive UHF frequencies, the opportunity to be received clearly and easily by cable, which now passes 90 percent of American households—though only about 60 percent of them actually subscribe to it.

The other great social and technological revolution of the 1980s was the video cassette recorder (VCR). In the home and in the classroom the VCR has had a massive effect on viewing habits. VCR penetration is now over 72 percent of all homes. A 1990 survey by Alexander & Associates reported that thirty-five million households are tuned to their VCRs at some time during prime time each week. On Friday and Saturday nights nine million homes (10 percent of all television households) are watching videos. Taken in conjunction with the impact of cable television, these statistics easily explain why public television lost some 12 percent of its audience between 1987 and 1991.

These developments are the most fundamental in the history of public television. What they add up to is that, a mere twenty-five years after its formal establishment, public television now finds itself part of a broadcasting environment that no one had envisaged in 1967.

Paradoxically (but in the light of events it is hardly surprising), these developments are not the ones that were given the most attention within public television in the 1980s. Attention was diverted for most of the decade to a more immediate problem—survival. The advent of the Reagan administration, its budget reassessments of 1981–83, its antipathy to federal funding of public broadcasting in general, and the eventual effects of the Gramm-Rudman-Hollings Act—these were the preoccupations of the CPB, PBS, and the stations throughout the decade.

Carnegie II had cited poverty as the principal problem of public television in 1978. Optimists could argue that total income had risen by 500 percent in ten years (but the baseline had been almost zero). Optimists could also argue that the authorization system and the "matching" formula were in place, and that this ought to give confidence for the future. Pessimists, on the other hand, compared the amount of money public television could afford for programming with the budgets available to commercial television—ABC's "Roots" spent $1 million an hour; "The Adams Chronicles," public television's glossiest and most ambitious homemade drama series, could spend only $500,000 an hour. CBS's "60 Minutes" was budgeted at $170,000 an hour in 1978; "The MacNeil/Lehrer Report" (as it was called in 1978) at $20,000. These were not exactly "like-against-like" comparisons, but they gave an idea of the disparity.

At first it looked as if the optimists would be right. Authorizations for public broadcasting voted by Congress for the years 1975–1983 rose from $65 million to $220 million, and public broadcasting's nonfederal income climbed even faster. But not even the pessimists had bargained for the tenacity of the Reagan administration. Appropriations for 1981–83 were rescinded. Between 1984 and 1986 there were no federal authorizations. Two such bills were vetoed in 1984, and in both cases the vetoes were sustained by Congress. The "matching" formula was inoperative. From 1981 to 1986 public broadcasters had to live with the very real fear that federal funding might be totally eliminated. In the end, bipartisan congressional support proved to be sufficient—but barely. It was not until 1989 that the actual appropriation for public broadcasting reached the $220 million originally authorized, and later rescinded, for 1983.

By the end of the decade it seemed that things were back on course, but with an awful lot of ground to be recovered. The Public Telecommunications Act of 1988 returned to the "normalcy" of three-year authorizations and set modest but reasonable targets. By this time, however, Gramm-Rudman-Hollings was in force, and the CPB, like every federal agency, became subject to sequestrations and rescissions in order to limit the overall federal deficit.

Federal funding has never been as important to public television (in terms of dollars, at any rate) as the support of state and local governments. In the early 1980s the states and localities did much to offset losses at the federal level, but as the decade wore on they proved unable to sustain the additional burden. More and more, public television had to rely on the private sector—and the private sector turned up trumps. Reagan administration supporters would argue that this was what they had planned for all along. A comparison of figures for 1981 and 1990 shows very clearly what had been happening during the decade:

+ The total income of public television, from all sources, was $626.1 million in 1981; by 1990 it had risen to $1.25 billion.

+ Federal funding, as a percentage, had fallen from 23.7 percent to 13.5 percent.

+ State and local government funding (including that from state universities and public colleges) had dropped from 35.3 percent to 29.5 percent.

♦   Private sector funding had risen dramatically, from 41 percent in 1981 to
    54.4 percent in 1990.

♦   Within this private sector funding, the two most significant advances
    were in subscription/membership (which had almost doubled: by 1990 it
    represented 21.9 percent of public television's total income) and corpo-
    rate underwriting (which had risen from 12 percent to about 17 percent
    of total income).

Thus, despite all the political infighting of the 1980s, and largely by its own
efforts and its own initiatives, public television had doubled its income during
the decade. There was a price to pay: the enormous amount of time and effort
stations now had to invest in fundraising activities diverted attention from
longer-term thinking and planning. Pledge weeks three times a year, and other
forms of on-air fundraising, were necessary; they were also a frequent source of
annoyance to viewers.

The increase in corporate sponsorship could be put down, in part, to the
activities of a body known as the Temporary Commission on Alternative
Financing (TCAF). At the beginning of the decade ten public television stations were authorized by Congress to experiment with paid commercials for a
period of eighteen months, under the supervision of the TCAF. When the
commission reported in 1983, it rejected commercials as a viable option for public television, but it urged the FCC to relax its rules governing on-screen identification of corporate underwriters so as to allow the use of brand names, trade
names, and slogans—all previously banned from public television. The FCC
accepted the recommendation, and in 1984 it authorized what became known
as "enhanced underwriting." It had an immediate effect, increasing income
from business and corporations from $38 million in 1983 to $56.6 million in 1984.
By 1992 it had risen to $90 million.

As was to be expected, "enhanced underwriting" caused (and continues
to cause) palpitations within the industry. In November 1991 the trade magazine *Broadcasting* expressed its fears:

> We know they're only "extended sponsorship credits," but somehow
> the difference between a 15-second sponsorship credit featuring,
> say, the name and logo of a car manufacturer and video featuring its
> latest sports car, and a 15-second commercial featuring the name and
> logo of a car manufacturer and video featuring its latest sports car,
> escapes us.[8]

What does not escape the audience, however, is that individual sponsorship or
underwriting credits are never longer than fifteen seconds and normally do

not intrude into programs. What *Broadcasting* and other critics of "enhanced underwriting" are probably more concerned about is the fairness or unfairness of commercial broadcasters having to compete for advertising/sponsorship against a government-subsidized competitor. They need not worry unduly. In 1992 advertising expenditures on commercial television in the United States are well in excess of $20 *billion*. In the same year, public television's total income from sponsorship/underwriting will be approximately $90 million.

With so much emphasis on funding and the business of survival, public television still had to grapple with its endemic organizational problems in the 1980s. As usual, these largely centered on the role of the CPB. There were various well-publicized "alarums and excursions." At one point a member of the board proposed an analysis of public broadcasting's entire output for political bias. The analysis never took place, but the proposal initiated a spectacular internal battle. At another point, when the chairman of the board intervened to stop a cultural exchange with the Soviet Union, the CPB's president resigned in protest; his successor lasted less than a year.

The underlying problem, given the political nature of the board, was the incompatible nature of the powers the CPB was expected to exercise—regulatory powers on the one hand, and creative programming responsibilities on the other. Regulation had always been the most important, and it had become more so as a result of the 1973 partnership agreement between the CPB and PBS, in which the CPB had agreed to send the bulk of its program funds direct to stations as Community Service Grants. Instead of itself directing the expenditure of that money, the CPB accepted that its role would be to monitor the stations' spending of it, and to ensure that it was spent in accordance with public policy.

During the 1980s, to the considerable gratification of those within the system (and to the growing horror of some outside it who felt public television's programming was unsupervised, unaccountable, and increasingly liberal in outlook), the CPB distanced itself even further from day-to-day control of programming. In 1981 a Carter appointee to the board successfully proposed that most of the remaining money earmarked for programming in the CPB's budget—after the Community Service Grants had been sent out to the stations—should be placed in a Program Fund that would be administered by the CPB's staff, not by its presidentially appointed board members. The board would establish priorities and policy directions—and it would, of course, appoint the staff responsible for administering the Fund—but it would surrender its "hands-on" authority. This mechanism continued to operate until 1988–89 when the CPB and PBS signed an altogether different contract.

In retrospect, it is possible to see 1988 as another landmark year in the history of public television—not because it resolved many of the system's problems, but because it set public television on a number of new courses, for good or ill. The Public Telecommunications Act of 1988 was by no means generous in the amount of federal funding it authorized for 1991–93 (annual increments of about 8 percent), but it compensated for this to some extent by giving public television an entirely separate grant of $200 million to purchase new and more powerful transponders on a satellite due to be launched in 1993, thus assuring public television's national "reach" for the next dozen years.

The Public Telecommunications Act also responded to the protests of independent producers, which had grown in volume during the 1980s. Many of them felt locked out of public television, which they saw increasingly as a preserve of white, middle-class, elitist producers, dominated by the big community stations in New York, Boston, Washington, and other cities. Along with a growing number of local citizen-activist groups, they argued that this was "public" television and that they should have a voice in it. The 1988 act included two provisions helpful to them. It ordered the CPB to set aside funding for the support of independent production, and to create and fund an organization that came to be known as the Independent Television Service (ITVS), with its headquarters in Minneapolis–St.Paul. Throughout the 1980s the CPB had devoted a significant proportion of its Program Fund (about 43 percent of it) to funding independent production. Now it was committed to allocating several million dollars each year (it was $7.5 million in 1991) to ITVS "in support of programs that involve creative risk." At the same time, the 1988 act formalized the CPB's long-standing support of programming by and about minorities. Administered through its Multiracial Programming Fund, this category of programming had taken an average of 21 percent of the CPB's Fund throughout the 1980s. Now, together with ITVS programming, it was a statutory requirement.

The Congress also handed down a specific directive to the CPB—to come up with a plan for the better distribution and deployment of its funding for national programming. As a result, the CPB produced *Meeting the Mission in a Changing Environment*—a plan for pooling the resources for national programming of the CPB, PBS, and the local stations. The plan was the genesis of what is known as the Chief Program Executive (CPE) model, the most radical and important development in public broadcasting in recent years.

The CPE model is explored in more detail in Chapter Four. Briefly, the model replaces the Station Program Cooperative. The SPC, founded in 1974, had allowed the stations to decide what programs to fund for PBS's National Program Service through a democratic series of proposals, presentations, and ballots. Now there would be a Chief Program Executive at PBS, in whose hands the stations would place their national programming money, and to which the CPB would add half the total value of its Program Fund—a grand total of approximately $100 million a year. Jennifer Lawson, who had previously been the director of the CPB's Program Fund, was appointed to run the new model. Thus, in a system securely based on localism and the primacy of the local stations, a dramatic move has been made to streamline and centralize the decision-making process for public television's most visible activity—its national programming. Decision by committee was replaced by the method used by every other significant network in the world—a program "czar." The CPB retains the right to reexamine the arrangement at any time. So do the local stations (which are, after all, the members and funders of PBS). No one in the system doubts that a great deal rides on the results of the experiment.

◆　◆　◆　◆

Today, twenty-five years after the passage of the Public Broadcasting Act, there is a wide perception that public television is in trouble. In point of fact, the immediate problems are not much worse than they usually are. But the long-term prospects are in need of urgent examination.

- *Reliance on federal funding*: Are there ways of doing without it or, if not, what is the justification for it, and are there ways in which it can be made more reliable and more long term?

- *Adapting to the new media environment*: How can public television harness itself and the newly available technologies to deal with a world in which electronic publishing is fast becoming as important as broadcasting?

- *Public television's own structure*: Parts of it are petrified and straining against change, other parts are desperately in need of nourishment and refurbishment. How can a locally based system of 351 different stations (some of them overlapping) maintain a strong enough national service to remain distinctive and necessary in the marketplace—necessary enough for more than five million people to subscribe some $280 million (which is what they do at present)?

These problems need to be addressed in the light of changed, and changing, circumstances.

- Instructional and educational broadcasting has to come into line with the new demands of teachers and students, precipitated by the availability of new technologies.

- The role of the local station has to be reconsidered in the light of new delivery systems and on the grounds of "mission effectiveness" as well as cost effectiveness.

♦   Public television's programming has to be looked at with an eye to com-
petitiveness and quality—quality above all, for that has been the watchword of public television from the beginning, and one that is unlikely to
let it down in the future.

A system created to fill an aching void in 1967 finds itself existing in
very different circumstances twenty-five years later. Part of the reason it is
under attack is that it has not yet shown how it is going to adapt to the new circumstances. Nor has it made clear what its mission will be.

Chapter Two

Technologies Old and New

Public television has an enviable record for making use of technological innovation—and for doing much of the innovation itself. It was the first American
broadcast system to have a nationwide satellite interconnection. Closed captioning
for the hard of hearing was developed by public television, which also pioneered
Digital Audio for Television (the so-called DATE system that gave us stereo sound
with pictures). A public television station (WGBH, Boston) developed the
Descriptive Video Service, a technology that makes programs accessible to the
blind by providing descriptions of the on-screen action on a separate audio
channel; this same technology allows programs like "The MacNeil/Lehrer
NewsHour" to be heard each evening in Spanish as well as English.

Some of these may seem small innovations (though they are not). They
are all examples of how television can be made available and accessible to the
largest number of people. Public television's major challenge in the 1990s is just
that—remaining available and accessible to the entire nation in the midst of
technological developments, many of which seem to conspire against public
television's traditional methods.

But not all traditional methods are going to be outdated. It is fashionable
among media pundits, for example, to proclaim the fast-approaching obsoles-
cence of terrestrial broadcasting (that is, over-the-air transmission of signals),
which is public television's principal method of delivery. This is a doubtful
claim in a country where 40 percent of all households do *not* subscribe to cable,
and where most households that do subscribe have several television sets, only
one of which is connected to the cable. Public television's over-the-air signal
reaches 94 percent of American homes (an additional 4 percent, out of reach
of terrestrial signals, can only receive it on cable or satellite feeds).

101

The next twenty-five years are not going to be substantially different from the past twenty-five years. The majority of viewing will doubtless be done on cable, just as it is today, but so long as cable costs money, which not everyone can afford, and so long as networks intend to be seen in every possible household, there will be terrestrial broadcasting.

Distance is no problem to public television because of the satellite link. As long ago as 1978 PBS pioneered the first nationwide satellite delivery service in American television. It leased (and later purchased) four transponders on the Western Union satellite, enabling it to send out four separate program feeds simultaneously to stations across the country. But satellites eventually run out of fuel and have to be replaced. The $200 million Satellite Replacement Fund voted by Congress in 1988 anticipated this. It allowed PBS to lease four transponders on an interim satellite, Spacenet I, when the original satellite ceased to operate in 1991. This is a purely temporary measure. In December 1993, AT&T will launch Telstar 401, on which public television will own six transponders—five of them in the wider "ku-band" (as opposed to the narrow "C-band" of the old satellite), which will enable stations to receive signals with greater fidelity, on much smaller receiving dishes, and at considerably reduced cost. Telstar is expected to have an operating life of twelve years (through 2005), and will make possible an enormous expansion of the service. Up to now each transponder has relayed a single feed: in the immediate future, with the advantage of digital signal compression, Telstar 401's transponders will each be capable of sending four, eight, maybe even ten signals simultaneously.

Even today, operating on the four "old-fashioned" transponders, the volume of public television programming distributed across the time zones is fairly startling:

◆   The National Program Service for five separate time zones (thirty-seven hundred hours a year)

◆   Four regional public television networks (forty-five hundred hours a year)

◆   Programs for individual stations and state networks (twenty-three hundred hours a year)

◆   The National Instructional Television Satellite, serving elementary schools in forty-two states (fourteen hundred hours a year)

◆   Other PBS educational services, including the Adult Learning Service, the Adult Learning Satellite Service, and the PBS Business Channel (fifteen hundred hours a year)

All this programming is transmitted on the satellite to the 175 public televi-sion licensees (who operate the 351 stations). All of them have "downlinks" to receive the signal, and nineteen of them also have "uplinks" enabling them to put programs into the system. The switch to Telstar 401 at the end of 1993 will hugely increase the system's capacity, enabling public television to become the carrier for educational and public service telecommunications organizations all over the country.

Getting the programs to local stations anywhere between Guam and the Virgin Islands is no problem. What is a problem is what engineers call the "last mile"—getting the signal from the local stations to the homes, schools, col-leges, and institutions served by the stations. Methods range from the state of the art to the downright primitive: terrestrial broadcasting, cable, microwave—even the bicycling of video cassettes. All this will change dramatically during the next few years under the influence of new technologies.

There are two principal developments that will be the engines of change. Both of them are already with us to some extent. The first is digitalization—the move from analog to digital transmission systems. Audio went digital in the 1980s, firing up the huge commercial success of the compact disc. Video is following behind.

In essence, a digital signal is transmitted in a succession of individual (or discrete) pulses, governed by a stream of ones and zeros, which indicate and control levels of light, color, and other values. It is more precise and more sophis-ticated than the analog system, which transmits information as a continuous signal, and therefore has much less control over quality. But even more impor-tant for public television is the fact that digital signals are capable of being high-ly compressed so that they take up less space in the spectrum and enable satellite transponders (for instance) to carry several signals simultaneously.

The second development affects the way telephone and television signals are delivered to our homes, classrooms, and workplaces. At the moment, most of these places are wired with copper and coaxial cables that do an efficient job, but they are being overtaken by the potential of fiber-optic systems. Fiber optics are thin, flexible fibers of glass and plastic that carry light and sound: a single strand can transmit hundreds of telephone messages and television sig-nals at very high quality. The huge capacity will not only expand our uses of communications (making interactive systems, for instance, much more read-ily available); it will also reduce the cost of communications in general.

What is happening at the moment is a patchwork and somewhat erratic introduction of fiber optics. Telephone companies (telcos) and cable compa-nies are installing fiber incrementally—that is, they are putting it in wherev-er it is cost effective. In the 1980s it cost substantially more than copper or coaxial cable, and there were technical problems associated with splicing fiber cables together. In the past few years the price has dropped, and it now makes sense to install fiber in the main trunks and, increasingly, in the "feeder" systems to streets near homes, schools, and offices. The final and most expensive stage—extending the fiber down the streets and into our homes, schools, and offices—has hardly begun.

The telephone industry is much larger than the cable industry and is proceeding at a faster pace. Statistics for 1990 show that 1.8 million miles of fiber were deployed in the United States that year—73 percent of it by telcos and only 5 percent by cable companies. But 1.8 million miles a year is still only a flea bite. At the moment, no more than 5 percent of the national telephone system is carried on fiber. Nevertheless, what is being built is, in effect, a backbone—what the telcos call a "highway system" of trunk lines and "feeder" systems. Eventually, the telephone companies and the cable companies will have the ability to rewire the country completely—a fiber-optic "one-wire supersystem" that will bring a fantastic array of services into our homes, offices, and workplaces: telephone, television, facsimile, data, video on demand, interactive services—all on the one fiber-optic wire. But in order to compensate them for the enormous cost of this venture (variously estimated at around $450 billion) the telephone companies insist that they must be freed from some of the restrictions of the 1982 Modified Final Judgment (the agreement under which the break up of AT&T occurred) so that they can provide video systems in homes. In July 1992, the FCC approved the use of Video Dialtone. This allows telephone companies to transmit, but not to produce, video programming in their own service areas.

The cable industry, meanwhile, has begun to develop an interest in fiber optics that was not much in evidence before 1989. Now, with lower costs and the frightening prospect that the telephone companies might be allowed into their business, they, too, are beginning to plan fiber-optic backbones for their systems. Wherever they face franchise renewals (or are bidding for entirely new franchises) it makes sense for them to offer "up-graded technology"—that is, fiber optics. Quincey, Washington; Omaha, Nebraska; and the borough of Queens in New York City are among the beneficiaries (residents of Queens, for example, will receive 150 channels, of which 60 will be devoted to pay-per-view movies). On an even bigger scale, the joint venture reportedly in negotiation between Time-Warner and IBM plans to own and operate a nationwide fiber-optic system to deliver interactive programming into homes. Such a scheme could outflank the telephone companies completely. There are many smaller, more localized plans of a similar nature.

Digitalization and fiber optics are likely to be the two great "enablers" of public television in the years ahead, but there is another technology that will also play a role. Direct Broadcast Satellite (DBS) services have already been operating for some years. They enable individual homes, apartment buildings, schools, colleges, businesses, and government agencies to receive signals directly from a satellite, circumventing local stations. Three percent of U.S. households (as high as 10 percent in rural areas like Montana) already have receiving dishes, getting their signals from existing high-powered satellite transponders. But satellite broadcasting is an expensive technology for serving individual customers, and although there are a number of commercial consortia reported to be planning more extensive services, it is likely to be a high-risk business. There are parts of public television's mandate, however, that can be (and in some cases, are being) served by low-powered DBS transponders using digitally compressed signals. Schools and colleges are the principal clients, often aided and abetted by state telecommunications systems and public television. Best of all, these DBS services (like fiber optics) are capable of providing interactive technology; they enable students to communicate with distant teachers, and they can provide video conferencing facilities to businesses, schools, and many other potential users.

Looking at the overall picture, it is possible to see how these new (or fairly new) technologies are expanding the capacity and capability of telecommunications and how, over the longer term, they are going to revolutionize them. Several states are already building, or planning to build, statewide telecommunications networks that will make use of satellite and fiber-optic technologies. Such systems are already under way in Indiana, Iowa, Kentucky, Maine, Nebraska, Oregon, and South Carolina. In many of them public television is acting as the coordinator or focal point:

- Nebraska's state legislature has funded the leasing of a satellite transponder that, with video compression, provides multiple feeds for the state's public television and radio stations, as well as state agencies and K–12 schools. The scheme, known as NEB*SAT, involves the addition of a fiber-optic network to provide local school districts with interactive classes.

- Iowa is constructing a 2,800-mile fiber optic network to cover the entire state. When it is completed in late 1993 it will connect Iowa's three universities, 15 community colleges, 11 private colleges, 8 public television stations, schools in all of Iowa's 99 counties, and government offices throughout the state.

- Maine, Vermont, and New Hampshire are all using fiber optics as well as microwave and T-1 telephone circuits to link educational institutions in interactive systems. An ambitious plan already exists to interconnect the three state networks in what is being called the Northern Tier Network.

In several other states, public television is involved in the planning or facilitating of new systems. There is activity almost everywhere, and as the recession recedes, the activity will increase.

Advances in satellite technology have also enabled some of the new services to be made available nationally, rather than just on a statewide basis:

◆ The Satellite Education Resource Consortium (SERC) is a joint venture of state public television systems and state departments of education. Created in 1989, SERC uses satellites to link rural and disadvantaged schools into interactive courses taught by specialized teachers from a distance. Students living in places where there are no teachers qualified to give courses in (for instance) Russian or Japanese, or advanced areas of the math and science syllabus, may still take these courses, thanks to the satellite and its interactive capacity.

◆ Ag*Sat, as its name implies, specializes in agricultural teaching and information. It links thirty-three colleges and universities to agricultural departments.

"Interactive" is the "in" word of telecommunications. Signal compression, DBS, and fiber optics are all contributors to its development—and so, of course, is the computer. PBS and the CPB have jointly funded an interactive computer technology known as VSAT (Very Small Aperture Terminal), which enables schools to send and receive voice messages, data, and images via computer and telephone lines. The technology was piloted by fifteen stations in the spring of 1992, and it is intended that every public television station in the country will be equipped with it by the end of 1993.

The people who are probably most in need of information about what these new technologies can do for them are teachers. They, especially, need information about what programs and courses (among the huge volume of educational television and video materials now available) would be most useful to them. A number of computer systems have been developed within public television to supply this information. Among them are the Learning Link, invented at WNET, New York, and Curriculum Connection, developed by WIVZ, Cleveland. Both of these systems are designed to give educators immediate access to resources supplied by public television.

New technologies and delivery systems will be of no value to public television unless it has access to them. Just as the FCC reserves 32 percent of over-the-air frequencies for noncommercial use, so it is necessary for parts of cable and satellite capacities to be reserved for public television. This is now guaranteed by law. The 1992 Cable Television Consumer Protection Act contains the necessary "must-carry" clause—a clear requirement that cable systems must carry all existing public television stations, as well as any that may come into existence in the future (provided their schedules do not duplicate those of existing channels that they overlap). The same legislation reserves 4 percent to 7 percent of DBS capacity for public telecommunications. For reasons that have little to do with public television, the "must-carry" provisions are now being challenged in the courts.

◆ ◆ ◆ ◆

All the delivery systems so far discussed in this chapter have been transmission systems of various kinds—methods of sending signals from one point to another. But public television, especially when it is wearing its educational hat, has to take account of other methods. Video cassettes, interactive laser discs, CD-ROM, and all kinds of computer software have become important tools. From the teachers' perspective, it is often more convenient to have prerecorded programs, which they can use in their own time and at their own convenience, than it is to be bound to transmission schedules not of their own making. Many schools now get their instructional programming (from both cable channels and public television) in the form of "block feeds" recorded on VCRs during the night, ready for teachers to use whenever they want during the day. And most schools are also investing in sophisticated video and computer programming, in much the same way that they buy textbooks. This is a major challenge to public television's more conventional methods—one that it is beginning to meet, but one that will require a very large investment if it is to be met head-on.

Nelson Heller, the publisher of the *Heller Report*, has estimated that between 1990 and 1994 the technology market in schools will grow at double the rate of the textbook market. The technology in question is largely video and computer programming, much of it being purchased on textbook budgets. Statistics supplied by Quality Education Data of Denver show that in 1992:

◆   U.S. schools average between three and four VCRs per school: only 2 percent of schools do not have a VCR.

◆   School districts that have authorized the use of video discs for teaching number 1,485 (representing 40 percent of the total student population). Schools that actually possess video discs total 6,502 (representing 5.8 million students).

◆   Just over sixty-seven hundred schools (representing 5.3 million students)are using CD-ROM.

Many people think that these technologies, together with the interactive compact disc (CD-I) which is only now being launched on the market, will be at least as important as broadcast programs to the future of education.

Textbook publishers are quickly moving into the education technology market, which is, after all, being fueled by textbook budgets:

- The Texas State Department of Education (second biggest budget in the nation) has approved the use of a video disc science curriculum throughout the state. Florida has introduced into its high schools an interactive video disc program on AIDS, which New York City has also purchased. California (the largest budget) and Kentucky have long-term plans to ensure that there are video disc players in every school.

- In late 1991, Philips Interactive Media launched the CD-I. Jointly developed with Sony and Matsushita/Panasonic, and therefore almost certain to become the industry standard, CD-I uses the same digital technology perfected in the audio compact disc. In a sense, the CD-I is computer and television/video player combined. There is more development to be done, but it is likely to have major ramifications later in the decade for both the retail and educational markets.

- The CD-ROM has also emerged as a significant teaching tool. Developed in the wake of the audio CD, CD-ROM (for "read only memory") is an optical disc technology for storing large amounts of data and reference works. Attached to a personal computer, it is now used as a teaching tool for purposes as varied as a reading tutor for very young children (*Cinderella* and *Peter Rabbit* are among titles recently made available), high school civics and public affairs classes (*Time* magazine's "Desert Storm" program was available to schools within three months of the end of the war), and the very sophisticated study of music (an annotated version of Mozart's *The Magic Flute*, for instance).

- CD-ROM players are comparatively cheap ($400). Because the software is cheap to produce ($2 per disc), and therefore highly profitable to manufacturers, traditional book publishers like Simon & Schuster have been quick to move into the technology. The capacity of a single disc is enormous—the complete works of William Shakespeare will fit comfortably on one.

None of this is based on prophecy; it is all happening now. Clearly, in order to maintain its position as a major educational resource, public television has to become a principal player in this new market—either on its own, or in partnership with commercial companies such as textbook publishers. A publisher possessing a ready-made distribution network would have a lot to gain from partnership with public television, and vice versa. Already, through PBS Video and PBS Home Video and through the initiative of a number of individual stations, public television is getting involved. But it will need substantial finance to get deeply involved.

◆ ◆ ◆ ◆

Digital compression, fiber optics, interactive satellite transmissions, CD-ROM, laser video discs—to some, all this may have a futuristic ring. But it is not the future: it is the present. Pundits from MIT's Media Lab and other reputable establishments tell us that what it all amounts to is the union of the television and the computer. Digital transmission will bring into our homes streams of information encoded in computer language (ones and zeros); it will arrive on fiber-optic cable (courtesy of the telephone company, no doubt) so that the volume of information arriving at any one moment is hundreds of times greater than the human brain can absorb. "Most information," says Nicholas Negroponte, director of the Media Lab, "will not be sent to people. It will be sent to machines." [1] (This comes as a relief to many of us.)

Before we too easily run away with this vision it is worth reflecting that neither the CD nor the VCR, nor even the personal computer, fundamentally changed our way of life in the past decade. The CD gave us better-quality music; the VCR was used mainly to play movies in the home; and the personal computer (for most of us) was either for playing games or a substitute for the typewriter. No more, in all probability, will fiber optics and digital transmission change our way of life in the 1990s. Some people, particularly the old and sick, will find it convenient to do their shopping from home via interactive television; most of us will prefer to go to the mall. Some people may decide that their entire home should be "on-line"; most of us will continue to reject the computer as part of the living room furniture.

Nevertheless, these developments will extend our horizons in many ways—particularly in the workplace and the classroom. Very soon a majority of the television audience will be computer literate. To the children of Nintendo, interactive video is a natural progression, easily absorbed.

By the time the twenty-first century begins we will probably be doing most of our viewing on high-definition television (HDTV), and a lot of it will be pay-per-view (PPV). These are the high-profile "glamour" technologies. Now that American industry has finally moved the HDTV argument into digital territory and away from the old-fashioned analog technology, which the Japanese and the Europeans had espoused with so much fanfare, it is likely that HDTV will develop into an important part of the television industry. It has not figured in this survey up to now because it is not a delivery system; it is merely a better picture—welcome, but hardly more than cosmetic. It is not in itself going to change the function or the capability of television and video.

What it will do (and public television has to be prepared for it) is raise the cost of program production in unacceptable multiples. In this respect, it is likely to carry more "cons" than "pros" for public television.

Much the same might be said of PPV. It is clearly a business that is going to grow as "dial-a-program" technology becomes more available. So far it has been most successful in two principal areas: events (mainly sporting events) and movies. In 1990 PPV grossed $135 million on events (of which $120 million was contributed by boxing and wrestling) and $130 million on movies. In the fall of 1991 New York's Metropolitan Opera put its Opening Night on PPV. Cablevision/NBC (which was also the PPV company responsible for the 1992 Summer Olympic Games) lost money on the venture and is not planning to repeat it in the near future. Nevertheless, for a "minority interest" like opera, the statistics were awesome: 34,000 homes bought the Opening Night feed at $34.95 apiece. Once sixty or seventy million homes are wired for PPV, then it will become an altogether more interesting proposition.

It is unlikely PPV will have much immediate impact on public television's principal areas of programming. What PPV almost certainly will do, however, is cut down, once again, the amount of time people spend watching broadcast television. A hit movie that can be dialed up straight into your own living room is powerful competition for broadcasters.

◆ ◆ ◆ ◆

There is a scenario shared by many of the leading thinkers in public television. It takes into account all these technological developments, large and small, and it acknowledges that public television's role has got to change—not so much its national role as its local role. The "last mile" problems will eventually be overcome by fiber optics and DBS and other methods—some of which will make the local station less essential as a distributor or middleman. At the same time, the requirements of schools and colleges and adult learners are changing, prompted by the availability of computer and video software that comes in the mail rather than over the air. So (the scenario says) the role of the local station must change. But any change must take into account the enormous resource that public television represents, as a nationwide infrastructure embedded in almost every community, with long experience of educational and instructional television, backed up by an enormous national resource, and with a deserved reputation for quality programming.

This scenario sees the local public television station developing into a Public Telecommunications Center, or an electronic local library, to which the entire community will have access. Local government, community associations, schools, colleges, and individual citizens all will make use of it. Essentially, it will be a multimedia center. It will continue to provide broadcast services; it will continue to supply instructional materials to schools (but often in the form of video and computer software); it will coordinate interactive services of all kinds from both within and without the community, for use in education as well as business and government; it will be a data center on the one hand, and a switching center on the other. All these roles it will combine with the more traditional one of being "the town square"—the community's notice board, its principal meeting place, the "amplifier" of its cultural institutions, and the focal point of community activities as diverse as drug prevention education and consumer advocacy. Outreach activities will be a crucial part of all this.

This multimedia public library, with its electronic town square, will have yet another dimension. It will continue to provide the community with a window on the world—the sort of window that commercial broadcasters and distributors will never be able to supply, for the very reason that it is not dependent on—or designed to fit in with—the marketing strategies of advertisers. PBS's national program service will thus certainly continue to be a major attraction of public television, but the strengthening of the local station's place and role in the community should mean that stations will no longer be as heavily dependent on national programming for fundraising as they undoubtedly now are.

Such a scenario fits neatly with technological and educational developments, so far as they can be foreseen. But there are some people within public television (and they are often the most successful) who argue that there is no sense in constructing scenarios—that the single greatest problem public television has is being thought of as a "system." These people argue that public television is not a system: it is 351 separate stations, and the only way to think of them is (as Dean Witter might have said) "one station at a time." We know more or less what CBS is; we may even know what Great Britain's BBC is; but what on earth is public television—other than a chronically overbuilt collection of stations that happen to be noncommercial? This school of thought opposes the idea of public television having a "mission": it is only interested in defining the function of each one of the 351 stations separately.

There are yet others who accept the electronic public library scenario, but only as a part of the definition. These people believe that a public television station certainly must serve its community, but not just in the somewhat passive way suggested by the library function. They put much more emphasis on the electronic town square element. They believe that public television stations must be proactive, that they must take the lead in attempting to solve community problems by putting their resources at the disposal of community groups and agencies that are addressing these problems, whether they be problems of health, violence, unemployment, illiteracy, or any of the other diseases that blight our country. These people are not so much interested in "outreach," which has been a traditional part of public television's activity, as they are in "inreach." There is no better example than the group of fifteen urban stations that have established themselves as the Nitty Gritty City Group.

There are, of course, other scenarios (including the one that says "We're doing fine: why change a good thing?"). But the electronic public library scenario may be worth bearing in mind, if only as a yardstick, as we examine the principal elements of "the system"—because public television's problems are not going to be solved in Washington. The key to change is the local station—always has been, always will be. If it cannot, or will not, change, then neither will public broadcasting.

CHAPTER THREE

"BY THE YEAR 2000. . . "
PUBLIC TELEVISION AND THE
NATION'S EDUCATIONAL GOALS

The briefest survey of public television would convince the most cynical observer that educational broadcasting remains what it has always been— the core of the noncommercial system. The volume of instructional, informational, and educational programming is awesome. What has detracted from it is not the commitment, which demonstrably increases year by year, but the perception.

It is arguable that when the first Carnegie commission coined the term *public television* it unknowingly did a disservice, because it concentrated the argument for federal funding on the prime-time schedule, which is just one part of the overall system. No one would deny the importance of national programming, especially when it comes to raising money from the private sector; but it equally cannot be denied that the concentration of attention on the national schedule, especially in congressional debates and hearings, has detracted from public television's principal claim for public support and public funding, namely that it is one of the greatest purveyors of educational resources in this country.

Public television is not intrinsically an educator in the sense that schools and colleges are. It is an "assist" to educational institutions—an additional resource for them to make use of. Television does not create curriculum; it provides programming to enhance the teaching and learning of a curriculum. It is not itself a policymaker or a course-setter (even when curricula are created around its own programs); those are the jealously guarded preserves of the genuine educational authorities—state departments of education, school boards, and college faculties.

That said, public television is, without doubt, one of the great "enablers" of the educational system in this country—a massive resource that is probably underused and certainly undervalued. You have only to go out into those states that truly value it (South Carolina, Kentucky, and Nebraska are random examples) to understand the power of the resource. And you have only to look at the new investment other states are pouring into it to begin to glimpse the potential of the twenty-first century. (For example, Iowa's statewide fiber-optic system, planned and coordinated by Iowa Public Television, will interconnect the state's 433 school districts, its area education agencies, its community and private colleges, and its three state universities.)

What is important—and what must surely be one of the clarion calls of public television in this decade—is that this huge resource exists as a nationwide infrastructure at precisely the moment that educational goals have been defined and promulgated by the president and the fifty state governors to put education back where it belongs—as a foremost national priority. It is not as though the wheel has to be reinvented; this enormous telecommunications resource already exists for educational purposes.

But (and it is a big "but") new technology is changing educational methods faster than at any previous time. Terrestrial broadcasting of instructional programming, which is the core of the public television system, while it is still very important, is being supplemented by other methods—cassette, laser disc, DBS, and other interactive technologies. Public television is reaching into these technologies, but it needs resources and funding to enable it to do so on the large scale that will be required in the years ahead. Cable distributors (to some extent) and textbook publishers (to a great extent) have seen this need and are moving quickly to provide for it. Public television—the producer of so much of the best educational programming available—cannot allow itself to be locked out of the new methods of distribution, any more than the nation can afford to allow that to happen.

And time is short.

◆   ◆   ◆   ◆

According to the goals presented at the 1989 education summit,[1] by the year 2000:

◆   Every child must start school ready to learn.

◆   High school graduation rates must increase to not less than 90 percent.

◆   Our students must be first in the world in math and science achievement.

◆   Every adult must have reading, employment, and citizenship skills.

◆   Every school must be a disciplined, drug-free environment.

Public television can make a critical contribution to the attainment of each one of these goals. Its instructional and educational programming is designed for lifetime learning; it covers the whole gamut of educational activities, formal and informal. It includes preschool, elementary, and secondary schools (K–12), college courses, adult education, adult literacy, teacher training, and vocational and job training—as well as a multitude of outreach activities. It has grown up as a mirror of the educational system, but also as a complement to it. It uses television and video as the main components, but it supplements them with print materials (teacher guides, newsletters, and promotional mailings), utilization workshops, video conferencing facilities, and (increasingly) on-line computer networks.

The programming itself is very definitely not of the "blackboard and pointer" variety so often caricatured in the past. Much of it is very sophisticated and of very high quality (including programs like Jaime Escalante's math series, "Futures," or Yale's "French in Action" series, filmed entirely in France and heavily dramatized). The following survey is necessarily partial and incomplete, but it gives a fair idea of the extent of the commitment.

ELEMENTARY AND SECONDARY EDUCATION PROGRAMMING

Instructional television (ITV) for K–12 students is the most extensive and most important part of the commitment. Two hundred and eighty-one stations (83 percent of the system) are involved in it. On average, they distribute 5.5 hours of ITV material each school day. Distribution methods vary.

Getting the programming to the local stations is no great problem. The favored method is through the National Instructional Television Satellite Schedule (NISS), which is a subscriber service masterminded by SECA (public television's southern regional network) out of Columbia, South Carolina. Subscribing stations in more than forty states pay an annual participation fee; in addition, they will pay license fees for those programs or series they decide to make use of. (Regional associations like SECA normally make "group buys" for their stations in order to cut down on the stations' paperwork and administrative costs.) Most of NISS's new programming each year is offered to stations in "block feeds" in July/August so that they can record it and fit it into their own daily schedules as is most convenient for their local schools.

For those stations that choose not to belong to NISS there are alternative methods. PBS's Elementary/Secondary Service (ESS) in Alexandria, Virginia, offers a feed, including a number of titles available at no charge (usually because they are underwritten by corporations). Some stations go in for the less exciting, but very straightforward, method of ordering the tapes direct from the producer or distributor, copying them, and returning the original.

All this is an efficient and well-worn system. Distribution problems are much more likely to arise in the "last mile"—getting the signal from the local station to the schools, colleges, and other users. Almost all the 281 stations involved in ITV use their primary broadcast channel as the main means of distribution. For about 60 percent of them, that will be cable. But many stations have found ways of augmenting this basic distribution. Some can make use of extra cable capacity. Some have the luxury of a second station or channel they can devote entirely to educational broadcasting. (OETA in Oklahoma, for instance, has its new Literacy Channel, which not only broadcasts instructional programs during the day but also enables working parents and their children to watch programs like "Sesame Street" and "Reading Rainbow" together in prime time.) Some fall back on the use of microwave Instructional Television Fixed Service (ITFS) feeds, which are reserved for educational purposes and enable stations to transmit programs direct to educational institutions that are equipped with a special antenna. (WNET New York/New Jersey, for instance, uses ITFS to send programs to correctional institutions, community colleges, and social service centers.)

More and more, schools like to receive ITV programs in the form of block feeds during the night. Preprogrammed VCRs record the entire block, so that teachers can use individual programs on video cassette in their own time and at their own convenience.

Even after the "last mile" has been conquered, there is yet another problem; public broadcasters sometimes call it the "last foot." This is the problem of getting the programs—whether they are broadcast, narrowcast, or on video—out of the central reception point in the school and into the actual classroom. Only one in four classrooms in this country is equipped with a television set. Almost no classrooms have telephones. Computers therefore tend to be laboratory equipment rather than classroom fixtures, and television and video are too often confined to the school library. Against that, one should put a survey of forty thousand elementary and secondary schools (nearly half of all the nation's schools) conducted by Market Data Retrieval in 1990–91. It showed that nine thousand of the schools surveyed used laser video discs, six thousand of them used CD-ROMs (mostly in the school library), and thirty-six hundred of them had satellite dishes in use. Twenty-four thousand of them (61 percent) were served by cable and were therefore able to make use of educational programming from cable channels as well as from public television.

Public television's own statistics show that almost thirty million students and 1.8 million teachers are in K–12 schools served by public television's ITV programming. A survey of a few (a very few) of the program titles currently on offer demonstrates the breadth of the service:

- "Futures": Jaime Escalante's innovative series for grades 7–12 showing how math relates to careers and jobs in the working world (produced by the Foundation for Advancements in Science and Education).

- "3–2–1 Contact": Children's Television Workshop's (CTW) daily science program for middle and upper elementary grades, balancing science content and entertainment to improve children's understanding of science.

- "Russian I" and "Russian II": credit-bearing high school courses offered by the long-distance satellite teaching service of the Satellite Education Resource Consortium (SERC) produced in South Carolina.

- "Japanese I" and "Japanese II": also offered by SERC and produced in Nebraska.

- "French in Action": a fifty-two-part half-hour romantic comedy shot entirely in France, each episode being followed by explanatory and illustrative sequences (produced by Yale University, WGBH, Boston, and Wellesley College, with Annenberg/CPB funding).

- "Genetics": three videos with accompanying computer software, supplied by Wisconsin Public Television.

- "The Voyage of the Mimi" and "The Second Voyage of the Mimi": the Mimi is a converted French tuna trawler outfitted as a modern ocean-going vessel. The episodes (produced by Bank Street College of Education in New York) feature a dramatic storyline interspersed with documentary science and math illustrations.

- "Amigos": introduces K–12 students to Hispanic culture and Spanish vocabulary (produced in Tennessee).

- "American Past": a high school series covering the period from colonial times to the Civil War, focusing on dramatic stories of individuals (produced in Denver).

These are just a few of the hundreds of the educational programs available to teachers. The Agency for Instructional Technology (AIT), based in Bloomington, Indiana, which is the largest single producer of K–12 programming (it has been in existence since 1962), lists 176 video series in its catalog alone.

All these series are designed specifically for use in schools, but there are other, better-known series that are broadcast as part of public television's national schedule—though they are very much a part of its educational effort for K–12 students. An appreciable (and increasing) part of the system's national programming resources are put into these programs. "Reading Rainbow" is an example—a program for kindergarten through third grade that continues to be funded each year as part of PBS's national schedule. On an entirely different level, "DeGrassi Junior High" might have been said to belong in the same category. So (much more obviously) might the new geography gameshow "Where in the World Is Carmen Sandiego?" It was joined in the fall of 1992 by a major new literacy series, "Ghostwriter," produced by CTW with cofinancing from the BBC. They are all part of a distinct movement of "national" resources (that is, the resources that fund public television's prime-time schedule) into programming for teenagers.

In addition, of course, few major series in the prime-time schedule are transmitted without some sort of educational and outreach package being made available to schools (often at the expense of the series' corporate and foundation underwriters—"Scientific American Frontiers" is an example: twenty million students and 165,000 teachers in grades 6–12 now use it). And PBS, through its Elementary/Secondary Service in Alexandria, is often able to negotiate off-air recording rights so that schools can make use of prime-time programs such as the "National Geographic Specials."

Nor is it surprising, considering the long-term market opportunities, that some of the most successful prime-time series have moved into the educational marketplace under their own steam—mostly by the application of new technologies. "Nova," for instance, has interactive video disc spin-offs. So does "The Civil War."

PRESCHOOL PROGRAMMING

Very young children have always been spectacularly well served by public television. "Mister Rogers' Neighborhood" was first broadcast in 1967, "Sesame Street" in 1969.

Unlike instructional programming for schools, which has separate and specific sources of funding, preschool programming is entirely the responsibility of PBS's national program schedule. Since the move two years ago to the Chief Program Executive model for managing the national schedule, there has been a conscious and conscientious effort to free up production money in order to reinvigorate preschool programming. "Mister Rogers' Neighborhood" and "Sesame Street" continue to be funded each year—as well as new episodes for each of them—but resources have also been deployed in the development of new series for 1992 and beyond. "Shining Time Station," "Lamb Chop's Play Along" (an interactive series using Shari Lewis and her puppets), and "Barney and Friends" (Barney is a large purple dinosaur; the series is set in a daycare classroom) have together been allocated more than $12 million of PBS funding in

1992 and 1993 (which amounts to the majority of all the monies to be spent on new programming, as opposed to continuing series, in those years). Another new series, called "The Puzzle Factory," will join the preschool lineup in 1994.

PROGRAMMING FOR TEACHERS AND CHILDCARE PROVIDERS

For children, television in the classroom is fun. For teachers it can be a nightmare. Teachers are the target for so much information, so many teaching aids, and so many commercial presentations that it is hard, if not impossible, to keep up with what is best and most useful to them. Public television tries to assist them in a number of ways. Those with computer skills can have access to Learning Link and Curriculum Connection, two very similar systems developed by public television stations to give teachers quick access to information about classroom resources. But even when they have located a video, or had a program recorded off air, it can often take a frustrating amount of time to find the right place in the tape. What they need is an index for each individual program— and that is what PBS engineers are about to supply them with. They are harnessing the unused part of the television signal (it's called the Vertical Blanking Interval—in layman's terms, the black bar you see when the picture rolls) to carry the necessary information. Teachers will access this Education Pipeline (as it is called) on a personal computer through a decoder box. It may sound complicated, but it will save hours of "fast forwarding" for teachers.

An altogether different way of helping teachers has been developed by WNET, New York, with funding from Texaco: the Teacher Training Institute for Science, Television, and Technology. In effect, this is a summer institute that gives elementary and secondary teachers hands-on training in the use of instructional television. The first institute, in 1990, emphasized science teaching and was attended by 250 teachers. In 1991, with additional support from the CPB, it was extended beyond New York to ten additional sites, and it now goes even farther afield.

Childcare providers are also catered to. Ralph Rogers (that same Ralph Rogers who, as chairman of PBS in 1972–73, fashioned the partnership agreement between PBS and the CPB that enabled public television to survive the Nixon veto) recently put together a Dallas-based consortium with CTW to develop the "Sesame Street Pre-School Education Program Project." PEP (as it is known) enables childcare providers to augment each individual "Sesame Street" program with art, play, and reading materials chosen to support the educational goals of the particular program. Thus, "Sesame Street" becomes an interactive, rather than just a passive, experience for children.

South Carolina ETV has developed an altogether different concept— "The Children's Place." Literally, it is a childcare center located on SCETV's own premises in Columbia, but it is also a production facility out of which a training series for childcare professionals is produced. In 1990 alone more than ten thousand video cassettes were shipped to people and institutions involved in

childcare, and in 1991 it added a facility for live video conferencing with childcare workers all over the country.

ADULT EDUCATION PROGRAMMING

As early as the 1950s, the City Colleges of Chicago became the first U.S.
college system to offer credit courses through television. Today the Colleges have
their own ten-year-old public television station, WYCC, whose purpose is
education. It has a weekly audience of 1.5 million, and more than ten thousand
students register with the Colleges each year to take credit courses by radio, television, and video.

Adult learning is part of the tradition of public television. In 1981 it was
focused and coordinated by PBS into the Adult Learning Service (ALS). It is
a self-supporting service, with colleges and universities paying a license fee for
the right to use ALS courses for credit. About two thousand colleges and universities use it, linked in local partnership with public television stations. In ten
years it has accumulated more than 1.7 million graduates, and millions more have
watched the programs at home for their own self-improvement and enjoyment.
The current ALS catalog offers fifty-one courses (all of them consisting of textbooks and study guides, in addition to television programs) in a range of subjects
from the arts and the humanities to business, science, and technology.

The way the partnership works is that colleges and universities, working
with ALS, select the courses they wish to use. The local public television station schedules the required courses, while the colleges and universities assign
faculty, collect tuition fees, select required readings, administer examinations,
and award credits according to their own standards. As a matter of interest, 68
percent of the students are female, 70 percent are between the ages of twenty-
three and forty-nine, and 14 percent are minorities.

A recent addition to the service is the Adult Learning Satellite Service
(ALSS). Unlike regular ALS, this is a nonbroadcast service that transmits
programs via satellite directly to colleges and universities, cutting out the local
station. About fourteen hundred colleges in the country have satellite receiving dishes, and about four-fifths of them make use of ALSS. Again, it is a self-
supporting service; colleges pay an annual participation fee of $2,500, plus
additional fees for individual courses and programs. They can (and do) make
use of the satellite to arrange live video conferences between themselves.

It was not coincidental that in the same year that PBS launched ALS
(1981), the Annenberg School of Communications and the Corporation for
Public Broadcasting jointly launched the Annenberg/CPB Project. A number of the telecourses found on ALS ("Ethics in America," "Mechanical
Universe," "Discovering Psychology," and "College Algebra" are examples)
were created by the project. So were many more courses designed for nonbroadcast technology. And many of the most successful prime-time public
television series of the past decade—series like "The Brain," "The Africans,"

"Planet Earth," and " The Constitution: That Delicate Balance"—were part-financed by Annenberg/CPB money to ensure that educational course materials would be created as an integral part of the production process. The project also created long-lasting and unique programs for students on campus; these were mainly computer and CD-ROM programs, such as Perseus (a massive encyclopedia of Greek civilization on CD-ROM and video disc).

In 1991 the Annenberg/CPB Project changed direction in two important ways. First, it moved from the creation of software for college and adult learners to a concentration on technology to help the "new majority learners" (defined as the 60 percent of all students who are likely to be pursuing adult education *outside* the classroom by the year 2000) to have at their disposal effective and practical technology. Second, the project shifted its program production emphasis—in accord with the president's and governors' educational goals—to improve the teaching of math and science through telecommunications and technology. For this purpose the Annenberg Foundation pledged $60 million over twelve years.

More than fifty million adult Americans do not have a high school diploma, let alone the opportunity to take college courses. For many of them, the General Educational Development test (known as GED) is their passport to employment—and "GED on TV," a series developed by the Kentucky Educational Television Network, is designed to help them obtain it. Public television stations in thirty-five states now use the series. A recent survey of "GED on TV" graduates showed that 54 percent of those who had been unemployed when they took the test were now working.

Even further down the educational totem pole are the twenty-seven million Americans who are functionally illiterate, and the thirty-five to forty-five million who are only marginally literate. PLUS (Project Literacy U.S.) set out in 1986 to make America aware of its literacy problem and to increase the nation's pool of volunteers involved in trying to do something about it. PLUS is a joint project between public television stations (led by WQED, Pittsburgh, in this instance) and Cap Cities/ABC. It has 450 local task forces and more than eighty thousand volunteers. Essentially, it is an outreach project; it uses television announcements and documentaries to further its cause, but most of the work is conducted by volunteers working on the ground in local communities. In the past three years it has moved its focus to young people and families, with a strong emphasis on mentoring (ONE PLUS ONE).

The nature of the workplace, once you secure a position in it, is that jobs change as new techniques and new technologies succeed each other. Constant retraining and upgrading of work skills is necessary. For this purpose PBS set up its Business Channel as part of the Adult Learning Satellite Service. The Business Channel creates resource programs for the workplace ("Managing Technology in the Global Marketplace," "Eye on the Economy," and so on) and organizes video conferences on subjects such as the future of oil and the requirements of the Clean Air Act.

The involvement of local stations in all these activities varies from very little to total immersion. WTVS in Detroit calls one of its channels "The Working Channel" and schedules it entirely with programs for adult workers. Wisconsin Public Television has enrolled fifty-nine thousand technical college students in vocational courses. WQED and WQEX in southwest Pennsylvania conceived "The Job/Help Network" in 1984. Public television is full of examples of such initiatives because every station should be, by its nature, keyed in to its own community.

Outreach activities play a very important part in these community relationships. Some of them are purely local and have little application elsewhere—but others can be shared between local stations and used widely across the nation. In 1985, with the help of the CPB, a Public Television Outreach Alliance (PTOA) was formed to provide a permanent structure for these initiatives. Through PTOA, national outreach projects have been established to tackle many different problems—drug abuse ("The Chemical People"), troubled youth ("Generation At Risk"), high school dropouts ("Sidewalk High"), AIDS ("America in the Age of AIDS" and "Stop AIDS!"), the environment ("Operation Earth"), the family ("The Family: All Together Now"), and several others.

◆ ◆ ◆ ◆

All this (and it is a very incomplete catalog) amounts to a massive commitment. But public television is by no means alone in the field. Textbook publishers like Simon & Schuster are quickly expanding their video publishing activities, and some of the most innovative uses of CD-ROM are coming from this area. Then there are satellite broadcasters, the most publicized of which is Whittle Communications, whose "Channel One" is a daily news bulletin (complete with commercials) sent by satellite to schools in many parts of the country. Whittle also supplies schools with free receiving equipment—a considerable incentive for schools to tolerate the commercials.

And there are the cable networks. In 1989 the cable industry established a nonprofit service called Cable in the Classroom. The service represents those cable companies and programmers who provide programs for schools. The programs are free of commercials, cleared for use in schools, and accompanied by the necessary support materials for teachers. Although the amount of this programming from individual cable companies is not very great (when compared to public television's, at any rate), the aggregate amount is not to be sneezed at. A few examples:

◆ A&E Classroom supplies an hour of "commercial-free programs with educational merit" Mondays through Fridays (7:00–8:00 a.m.); a different subject area is covered each day—history on Mondays, performing arts on Wednesdays, and so on.

- Black Entertainment Network supplies a two-hour block biweekly on Fridays called "Teen Summit."

- C-SPAN produces "Short Subject", a ten-minute weekly series examining how government works. It also provides teachers with "C-SPAN in the Classroom," a service that encourages teachers to use C-SPAN's regular programming for teaching purposes.

- "CNN Newsroom," like Whittle's Channel One, is a daily fifteen-minute news bulletin—but without commercials.

- "Assignment Discovery" is a one-hour daily program consisting of two documentary segments customized for classroom use.

- Nickelodeon broadcasts four programs a week for use in schools—"Launch Box," "Eureka's Castle," "Kid's Court," and "Kidsworld."

- The Learning Channel devotes 37 percent of its airtime to instructional programming, some of which is secondary distribution of programs (including a number of Annenberg/CPB projects) already seen on public television.

An important development for Cable in the Classroom is the acquisition of one of its newest members—public television. Long-range plans call for the building of partnerships between local cable companies and public television stations in order to develop workshops for educators all over the country. For public television, the alliance would appear to make sense because there is no escaping the increasing importance of cable as a delivery system for instructional television.

Meanwhile, the cable companies are earning dividends from their involvement in educational television. It has brought them public relations benefits in places where they matter; it probably helped in the campaign to keep regulation at bay; and it has enabled the industry to set a target (and to come close to meeting it) of having 100 percent of American schools cabled by the end of 1992.

Nevertheless, to put things in their proper perspective, the cable industry's total involvement in education is tiny compared to public television's. A 1990 survey of teachers by A&E showed 56 percent of teachers assessing public television as "the top source of educational programming," with A&E itself having the next best rating at 16 percent.

◆ ◆ ◆ ◆

Public television has two enormous strengths in educational broadcasting: the quality and quantity of its programming, and its representation in almost every local community in the country. It is, first and foremost, a producer. But producing is of little use if you cannot also publish—or be published—in a form acceptable to the market and capable of effective distribution. It is in this respect that public television has to plan for the future.

The importance of public television's programming in education is not diminishing. It is increasing. But delivery systems are changing, and public television must have the resources to change with them. Much of the new satellite capacity becoming available in 1993 will be used for educational programming—a Math Channel, a Science Channel, an Adult Education Channel, a Literacy Channel, and others, it is hoped. New channels will need additional programming.

At the same time, public television needs the money and resources to diversify its distribution methods—to be able to adapt and create programs in formats that are more and more favored by teachers and students: video cassette, video disc, CD-ROM, and computer software of all kinds. These are the materials local stations will have to have at their disposal if they are to be electronic public libraries in their own communities. Major producing stations such as WGBH, Boston, are already putting resources into this effort; in Nebraska public television has established a center for video disc training and production; PBS Video (a division of PBS itself) has been created to distribute video cassettes to educational institutions. The system seems to be ready to move forward—but it lacks the means.

If public television is to realize its true potential in helping to attain the nation's educational goals by the year 2000, it will need additional resources. The 1994–96 Reauthorization Bill, which provides for quite substantial increases in federal funding, is a beginning. According to testimony from public television officials, these increases are earmarked largely for educational needs:

◆   Developing new K–12 programs

◆   Enhancing preschool programming

◆   Expanding community service activities

◆   Creating citizen awareness

◆   Addressing adult literacy problems

These are the priorities of public television in its role as a program producer of educational programs. But it must also be a publisher and disseminator of its programs, and these are processes that must also be given high priority in the immediate future.

Chapter Four

Programming

F rom the beginning, public television programming was designed to fill a gap in the coverage provided by commercial television. To begin with, in the 1950s and early 1960s, educational television was the sole objective. But with the encouragement of the Ford Foundation, and the eventual involvement of the first Carnegie commission, a much wider brief was designed. Cultural programming and public affairs programming were the first priorities. Then Children's Television Workshop (CTW) made children's programming into public television's first popular success. Shortly afterward, in the 1970s, most of the "pillars" of the system were created: "Masterpiece Theatre," "Great Performances," "The MacNeil/Lehrer Report." By the early 1980s it was possible—indeed, easy—to argue that public television had successfully plugged the gap in the commercial networks' coverage: there was "Nova" and "Nature" and "American Playhouse" and "Wonderworks" and "Wall Street Week" and "Frontline" and "National Geographic Specials," and a host of other titles that were part of the American consciousness.

Then came the cable networks, many of them hoping to colonize the "niches" public television had made its own. Nickelodeon and Disney aimed at children, FNN and CNBC at business, A&E and Bravo at culture, CNN and C-SPAN at public affairs, the Discovery Channel and the Learning Channel at documentaries. Public television's programming was no longer so exclusive. Cable networks even began to inhabit that supremely noncommercial area— educational television. What this process revealed was something that had been unthinkable at the time of public television's founding: these "niche" areas of television were, after all, commercial, and they had been made so by the evolution of narrowcasting, as opposed to broadcasting.

So now the question that has to be asked is whether there is any need for public television any longer.

One quick (and not so facile) answer might be to point out that more than five million individual citizens each subscribe an average of more than $50 a year to their local public television stations in order to support the institution. One could also point out that only about 60 percent of American households subscribe to cable—while 98 percent can receive public television. And there are other obvious attractions: public television's direct relationship with its local communities, its uninterrupted programming, its huge investment in educational broadcasting, and (above all) the quality of its programming.

There is clearly an audience for public television, and a substantial one. The Nielsen Television Index for 1990–91 shows 54 percent of all American television households watching public television at some time each week (that is about eighty-seven million people). Slightly fewer (about forty-five million) were watching in prime time at least once a week.

Most people assume this is some sort of "elite" audience. In fact, it is not. Demographics published by public television show that it is a remarkably faithful mirror of the population of the United States (Figure 4.1).

FIGURE 4.1
COMPARISON OF PUBLIC TELEVISION AUDIENCE WITH ALL TELEVISION VIEWERS

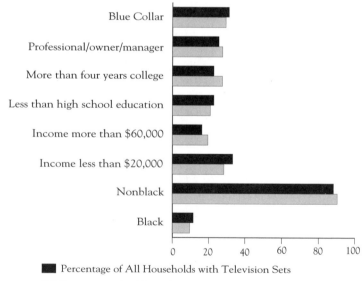

Source: APTS Facts File, 1991. These demographics reflect *all* public television viewing: prime-time statistics alone would reflect a somewhat more "upscale" audience.

The most widely accepted measure of audience size in the television industry is the audience rating, which is expressed as a percentage of all available television households. Public television's average prime time audience rating for
1990–91 was 2.2. This compares with 1.0 for CNN (in a year that included the
Gulf War), 0.6 for the Discovery Channel, and 0.4 for A&E. Public television's
highest annual rating (2.7) was in 1986–87. Since then its ratings (in common
with all U.S. broadcasters) have gradually decreased in response to the cable
and VCR booms. For the time being the process appears to have leveled off, but
it would be prudent for broadcasters to assume that there will be further erosion
in the years ahead as homes acquire a multiplicity of alternative sources of
entertainment and information—pay-per-view movies, Direct Broadcast Satellite
feeds, interactive video systems, etc. (Once again, the scenario of the local
public television station as an electronic public library comes to mind. If public television is capable of adapting to some such role it could become a beneficiary of change, rather than a victim.)

LOCAL PROGRAMMING

It is impossible to get codified information about the local programming
activities of 351 individual stations, but local production is certainly the biggest
and most expensive activity of public television.

"Local production" includes a number of different activities, of which
the actual production of local programs is just one. It also includes the rescheduling of PBS's national program feed to meet local needs; the acquisition of programming from other sources (mainly public television's regional networks); and
the stations' outreach activities within their own communities, in which they
are increasingly able to integrate centrally produced materials with their own
local contributions. A Boston Consulting Group (BCG) study, commissioned
by the CPB (and explored in more detail in Chapter Five) estimated that the
total cost of local production in 1989 was $570 million (about 43 percent of pub-
lic television's total expenditures). Of this amount, $100 million was account-
ed for by the costs of rescheduling PBS's national feed (including the cost of
acquiring replacement programs where this was considered necessary). The
remaining $470 million was the cost of local program production, including stu-
dio and overhead costs as well as outreach activities.

The BCG study estimated that local production accounts for only 7 percent of public television's total broadcast hours—and easily its biggest investment in resources, both capital and human.

There seem to be no reliable statistics for the amount of local programming
produced by the stations. The CPB estimates that it has been "gently declining" for a decade; in the past two years, in response to budget cuts, the decline
has become much more marked. Exceptional stations originate more than two
hundred hours a year; the average station, it seems, produces a little more than
one hundred hours. The programming varies from local news programs, talk

shows, and community billboards, to sophisticated documentaries and even (in very exceptional cases) dramas. A number of statewide licensees produce regular live coverage of their legislatures. Oklahoma ETA (highly exceptional) produces a half-hour news program every weekday; a business program, a wildlife show, and separate programs about Tulsa and Oklahoma City—all of them weekly; OETA also provides live coverage of the state legislature, adapts and syndicates old Lawrence Welk shows for about 90 percent of all public television stations, and in 1989 it produced a fully dramatized all-film five-part miniseries on 150 years of Oklahoma history seen through the experiences of one family. Oklahoma ETA is exceptional! At the other end of the scale there are stations that do little more than pledge-week fundraising.

Ratings for locally produced programs are mainly between 1.0 and 1.5 (half the prime-time ratings), but, again, there are exceptions: WTTW, Chicago, and KAET, Phoenix, regularly record ratings in excess of 2.5.

However one looks at them, the statistics are not favorable to local production, at least not in terms of cost effectiveness. But that is not the context (certainly not the *only* context) in which they have to be seen. Localism is more than just a convenient philosophy for public television; it is a very practical matter, for it is at the local level that the bulk of the funds for public television are raised. The question posed by the statistics is not whether localism is good in itself, but of what does localism consist? For the vast majority of stations it would appear that locally produced programs, *per se*, are not of the essence, since most of them are viewed by only about 1 percent of the audience. Fundraising programs, on the other hand—pledge drives, auctions, and festivals—are very much of the essence; they are the *sine qua non* of public television.

Questions are also asked about the nature of the programming purchased by local stations as part of their rescheduling operations. The legislative record of the 1988 Public Telecommunications Act noted that "some public television stations are increasingly turning away from traditional public, educational and informational programming and broadcasting . . . such programs as 'Disney,' 'The Avengers,' 'Lassie,' 'Ozzie and Harriet,' and 'Star Trek.'"[1] A more recent and widely quoted example is "The Lawrence Welk Show."

All these programs (and many more) are purchased by local stations in order to boost their ratings and, as a consequence, their subscription income. There is evidence that it works: a "Lawrence Welk Special" is listed in the top twenty most popular public television programs of all time, alongside "National Geographic Specials," and "The Civil War." Nevertheless, the legislative record of the 1988 act made it clear that the Congress "was concerned that public broadcasting, in an effort to secure alternative financing and to increase ratings and viewership, is sacrificing its identity and uniqueness."[2]

All this gives rise to a number of tough questions, none of which will be popular with the local stations, but all of which have been asked before. They have an added urgency today because of the need to strengthen the national schedule in the face of growing competition, because of the steadily changing technology on which telecommunications are already coming to depend, and because of the need to increase the effectiveness of local stations as the hub and mainspring of the public system.

The BCG study was armed with a Project Steering Committee consisting of twenty people drawn from different areas of expertise within public television. The published report was prefaced by an introduction written by the Steering Committee (not the BCG people) as a "User's Guide to the BCG Study." Conscious of the provocative nature of the study's conclusions, the Steering Committee addressed itself to station managers and listed a number of questions (or "Provocations," as it called them) that should be taken seriously. Among them were the following:

- Is it necessary for local stations to *own* production facilities?

- What if Community Service Grants from the CPB could not be used for local-only activities?

- If local program costs were cut by reducing the production complexity of programs, would the audience for these programs necessarily decline? If 99 percent of the audience failed to tune into them, instead of 98 percent, would that matter?

- Are the complex, labor-intensive means of production used by most stations still necessary? Despite union agreements and traditional staff hierarchies, are there still ways of "downsizing"?

- How much of the commitment to studio production facilities is driven by the needs of on-air fundraising and/or auctions?

- What if commercial stations in the same market had an interest in sharing local production resources?

- Is it possible or desirable to direct some of a station's program resources away from purely ephemeral broadcasting and into programs or projects with a longer "shelf life" and of longer-term use to the community?

- In view of technological and other changes, should stations be considering new methods of fundraising, some of which might not be dependent on the use of a broadcast transmitter?

- Might the $100 million a year spent on rescheduling the national PBS feed be better spent in providing other services to the community?

◆   Could nonoverlapping stations combine their program operations and
     on-air promotion functions—and even some of their programming?

◆   Is it possible to exploit more effectively the local value of "national" pro-
     grams, and to reinforce the role of the local station as the agency providing
     that service?

◆   Why don't stations follow the example of some of their commercial col-
     leagues by establishing cooperative ventures to distribute centrally or
     regionally produced programs (Group W's "PM/Evening Magazine" is a
     shining example) that can be effectively "localized" by each station by
     adding its own presenters, and by including one or two purely local items
     of its own?

◆   Rather than competing with, or duplicating, educational and instruc-
     tional programming supplied by cable and satellite companies, should
     not public television stations concentrate at least some of their resources
     on complementary activities—such as providing utilization services to
     accompany cable feeds?[3]

As the Steering Committee rightly said, these are "provocations." It is possible for every station to reject *some* of them for the soundest of local reasons.
But the fact remains that local production and local rescheduling of the national feed are costing the system a quite unjustifiable proportion of its income. The
key to change lies with the stations. If they are prepared to rethink their role
and their activities in the light of changing circumstances—social, technological, educational—and in the light of the changing media environment,
then it is highly likely that the results could be beneficial to them, as well as
to the system as a whole. They could certainly play a bigger and more effective
role than they now do on the local scene, while making a bigger contribution
to the national scene.

    None of this is meant to deny the existence of some very effective local
stations. Most of these stations reflect facets of public television that are not too
visible when you look at the national schedule. Multiculturalism is one of them.

    Multiculturalism has always been a part of public television's mission.
"Black Journal" (still on the air as "Tony Brown's Journal") was the first series
ever to receive CPB funding back in 1969. Two series of "Eyes on the Prize,"
"Civilization and the Jews," and a number of individual programs (the film
Stand and Deliver, shown on "American Playhouse," is a prime example) have
dealt with multicultural subjects in the national schedule, but not very frequently. Since the recent change to the Chief Program Executive method of
managing the national schedule, there has been a much greater thrust in the
multicultural direction, especially in PBS's long-running and continuing series.

But for local stations, which are required to reflect their own communities, multiculturalism has always been a major commitment. "Black Horizons" in Pittsburgh, "Say Brother" in Boston, "Detroit Black Journal," "Images/Imagenes" in New Jersey, and "Mundo Hispano" in Bethlehem, Pennsylvania, all date back to 1975 or earlier, and all are still on the air. Many stations across the nation can boast similar commitments. KBDI in Denver, KMPT in San Francisco (which is under multiethnic control), and WHMM in Washington, D.C. (owned and operated by Howard University) are programmed specifically for minority audiences.

It is not just through their on-screen programs that local stations address the multicultural problems of their communities. Outreach activities play an important part. KERA in Dallas provided a famous example in 1989. Concerned by the racial antagonisms visible in the city, KERA launched Project Crossroads—a successful effort to persuade fifty mainly white church congregations to pair with, and mix with, fifty nonwhite congregations. Out of the project came eleven special programs and a mountain of publicity and praise. In a similar initiative, WTVS, Detroit, is currently using its electronic resources to link up two thousand church congregations dispersed over 140 square miles of concrete (if one may so describe Detroit).

NATIONAL PROGRAMMING

The National Program Service is provided to the stations by PBS from its headquarters in Alexandria, Virginia. PBS is not allowed by its bylaws to produce or make programs itself. It buys or commissions them and then distributes them to the 351 stations on its daily satellite feeds—a total of twenty-eight hundred hours of programming a year, of which fifteen hundred hours are new and unduplicated.

For seventeen years, up to and including 1991, national programming was largely dictated by a very democratic-sounding organization called the Station Program Cooperative (SPC). Each year, in a series of proposals, presentations, and ballots, the stations would decide which national series they would fund. The SPC rarely, if ever, provided all the funds necessary to produce a series, and failure to win SPC funding did not necessarily disqualify a series from getting into the national schedule. Alternative and additional sources of finance (such as corporate and foundation support, or international coproduction) might be available. But the SPC provided a large proportion (normally a bit less than half) of the total funding available to PBS for the compilation of a national schedule.

The SPC may have been democratic—in the sense that it enabled the stations to confront and question producers of major series, and eventually to support (or not to support) those series with their funds—but it was also very cumbersome. It lacked flexibility (over the years there were comparatively few changes in programming), and it was notably unresponsive to the marketplace, especially in matters of pricing and production costs.

In 1988 a series of discussions took place within public television. Late in 1989 they gave birth to the proposal that the National Program Service should be managed by a Chief Program Executive (CPE). Jennifer Lawson was appointed to head up the executive. Although she took over the scheduling of the service immediately, 1992 was the first year in which she has had a substantial impact on the overall shape and content of the programming; 1993 will be the first year in which the schedule is entirely her own.

The effect of the CPE model is to move from a committee system to a program "czar"—in other words, to come into line with the practice of almost every other television network in the world. All national programming monies from within public television—from the stations and from the CPB—are effectively placed in the hands of one person—over $100 million a year. Lawson has appointed a National Program Service Advisory Committee to help her—but the responsibility is hers. The new model also, very importantly, gives her control of the promotional budget for the National Program Service.

A number of results can already be seen:

- The national schedule is clearly more flexible and more responsive to change. In the four years 1988–91, the old SPC system had failed to eliminate a single continuing series; by 1991 there were thirty-three of them being funded by the SPC. For 1992, the new CPE system eliminated seven of these series and introduced eight new ones; in 1993, six more series have been discontinued.

- The chief beneficiary of these changes has been children's programming. "Lamb Chop's Play Along," "Barney and Friends," "Shining Time Station," "Where in the World Is Carmen Sandiego?" and "Ghostwriter" have all been added to the schedule.

- The Gulf War enabled the CPE system to demonstrate how swiftly and effectively it can respond to events; approximately $1 million was spent by the CPE on some thirty special programs. The Clarence Thomas hearings demonstrated the same ability to preempt and reschedule at short notice. On Sunday, October 13, 1991, one station (KAET, Phoenix) registered a remarkable prime-time rating of 17.7 (a 27 share). The national public television rating that evening was 12.2 (about ten points above the average).

- More of the continuing series are including multicultural programs ("Great Performances," for instance, includes programs on rap, dance videos, and Hispanic culture).

- There has been a very marked increase in the percentage of stations committing to full participation in the National Program Service. In 1991 it was only 59 percent, whereas in 1992 (the first effective year of the CPE model) it rose to 82 percent; it will drop back to about 80 percent in 1993. (The remaining stations opt for reduced participation under a limited-use discount scheme.)

- This increased participation has not led to an expanded budget for national programming. Rather, it has held down the contributions of the participating stations—at a time when state and university budgets, on which many of them are heavily dependent, are being savagely cut. The stations' aggregate contribution to national programming went up steeply between 1987 and 1991 (the last years of the SPC), with annual increases ranging from 17.5 percent to 10.9 percent. For 1992 and 1993, the equivalent increases are 3.1 percent and 3.6 percent, respectively.

- Some progress has been made in the areas of advertising and promotion, which are now also controlled by the CPE. "Showcase Weeks" and "Back to School Weeks" at the beginning of each season have generated good publicity. The Hal Riney & Partners Agency has been hired to develop a more coherent image and identity for public television, while the Fleishman-Hillard agency is developing messages on the value of public television and helping stations to position themselves to best effect.

All these developments are positive signs, but they will not be worth the paper they are written on if the national schedule fails to generate increased revenues. This means increased corporate and foundation support where possible, but most of all it means "viewers like you"—individual subscribers who will pledge contributions year after year. The vast majority of them make their contributions because of the national schedule. If it declines in quality or popularity—or if, in changing, it proves less attractive to existing subscribers but more attractive to people *un*willing or *un*able to make pledges—it will be a catastrophe for public television.

There are many people within the system who welcome the increased flexibility the CPE has already demonstrated. They welcome brave decisions like the funding of "Where in the World Is Carmen Sandiego?" (an adventurous format that would not have won easy approval from the National Endowment for the Humanities), and they welcome the competitive edge the CPE is proving it can give them by committing major funding to international coproduction opportunities years in advance (WGBH's recently announced $15 million twenty-six-hour series with the BBC, "The People's Century," is a good example). But these people worry, too. They worry about delegating so much influence to so few individuals; they worry that the CPE is not attuned to helping major producing stations leverage additional (and essential) support from corporations and foundations; and they worry, most of all, about the core constituency of public television—its traditional audience.

This is the heart of the problem. There is a very clear division within public television—a division of taste and mission. There are those who believe passionately that the core constituency requires public television to be guided always by qualitative, not quantitative, measurements. And there is a group of program managers, recently in the ascendant, who believe that quality and quantity are not incompatible, and that ratings can be substantially increased without harming the core constituency: Indeed, they believe that that constituency can, and must, be expanded. The CPE finds itself at the junction of this dichotomy, appearing to favor the latter view, but with no immediate means of knowing if it can succeed—or what the consequences will be if it does not.

The acid test is likely to come as the CPE embarks on its next priority (after children's programming and multiculturalism), which is the problem of 8 P.M. scheduling. Public television's existing 8 P.M. series are quite narrow in their appeal. The objective is to find some more broadly popular series that will deliver a bigger audience for the rest of the evening. PBS and the CPB have earmarked $6 million from the 1993 Program Challenge Fund (which they jointly administer) to tackle this problem, with the promise of further funding in 1994, but it will take a lot more than that.

In an election year—never more so—public television programming is bound to be susceptible to partisan attacks from left and right. PBS's official policy is to strive for fairness in every program and for balance over the course of the entire schedule. For "Election '92" PBS was offered, and rejected, the opportunity to do something completely new—something that had been devised outside public television, at the Markle Foundation, and that would have been partly underwritten by a $5 million grant from Markle.

In 1989–90 the Markle Foundation had independently financed a feasibility study. It came up with a document called *The Voters' Channel*—a proposal for about twenty-six hours of election programming on PBS. It included an innovative "free-time" idea that would have offered air time to the major presidential and vice-presidential candidates, and/or the parties, "to communicate directly with the electorate so as to encourage rational advocacy"[4] (a proposal that would have needed clearance from the FCC, or even a change in Section 315 of the 1934 Communications Act—the "equal-time" doctrine). Air time would also have been given to "The Voice of the People," enabling individual voters "to articulate and express their feelings and concerns."[5] Much of the production (according to the Markle study) would have been done by independents, along with public television's major producing stations. The estimated budget was $12 million—of which Markle would provide $5 million, PBS would contribute the $3 million it had already budgeted for election coverage, and the remaining $4 million would be raised elsewhere.

There were a number of problems along the way and PBS eventually made a decision not to proceed. It is possible that there may have been a perception in some parts of the system that, while $5 million was a generous contribution, it still meant having to accept a scheme manufactured outside public television—and that (these people thought) was too high a price to pay. There were others who felt it was an innovative scheme that would reinforce public television's reputation as the network of record—and that it had rejected it to its own detriment. Whatever the reasoning, it was an awkward beginning to the election process because of the bad publicity it generated—and because of the subsequent announcement that Markle had moved the project to CNN. In the end, public television's election coverage, bereft of *The Voter's Channel*, received plaudits for its convention coverage in collaboration with NBC News, and criticism for placing much of its remaining campaign coverage in the hands of Bill Moyers and William Greider, perceived by some journalists and other critics as having a "liberal bias."

No broadcaster in history, whether commercial or noncommercial, has succeeded in always being unbiased and always being totally fair. The Fairness Doctrine, which required broadcasters to devote reasonable amounts of time to the discussion of controversial issues of public importance and to do so fairly by affording time to opposing viewpoints, was swept aside in the 1980s. First Judges Robert Bork and Antonin Scalia reinterpreted the doctrine in the Circuit Appeals Court, then President Reagan vetoed a bill designed to overrule Bork and Scalia. At the present time, the doctrine appears to be in some kind of suspension. But not (in effect) for public broadcasters. They depend on politicians for part of their funding; it follows that they will always be under intense scrutiny so far as "balance" and "fairness" are concerned. Moreover, they have learned the hard way that scrutiny easily turns into attack—normally, but not always, from the conservative wing. Robert MacNeil and Jim Lehrer, Bill Moyers and William Greider, and other PBS regulars are alleged to be liberal; the balance provided by William F. Buckley, John McLaughlin, and others is deemed insufficient.

At the same time (and very often as part of the same argument), conservative critics accuse public television of including in its schedules programs of a less political nature, but that nevertheless display a liberal bias in social and moral ways. Recent controversies have surrounded the decision to present "The Lost Language of Cranes" (with strong homosexual content) on "Great Performances" as well as a documentary about gay blacks, "Tongues Untied," which was included in the series "P.O.V." As it turned out, only 174 out of the 284 stations that normally carry "P.O.V." transmitted "Tongues Untied." And barely a month later PBS and "P.O.V." were under attack again—this time from the other direction—for their decision *not* to air a documentary called "Stop the Church," which recorded the 1989 occupation of St. Patrick's Cathedral in New York by the activist group ACT UP.

There will be more controversies in the future. Intense speculation surrounds the list of Independent Television Service (ITVS) projects from independent producers, which are part-funded by CPB money mandated by the 1988 Public Telecommunications Act. Titles include "Endangered Species: The Toxic Poisoning of People of Color" and "Warrior: The Case of Leonard Peltier." (The Peltier case has already been the subject of a "60 Minutes" segment as well as a full-length documentary by Robert Redford and Michael Apted.)

While most of the current, and most audible, criticism has come from conservatives, public television is under continuous pressure from the liberal wing as well. Liberals have concentrated their criticisms not so much on the content of individual programs as on the absence from the schedule of minority voices: women, Hispanics, Native Americans, African Americans and others.

Aside from public television's internal studies of these issues, the only detailed analysis has come from a conservative source, the Center for Media and Public Affairs in Washington. In March 1992 it published a report, *Balance and Diversity in PBS Documentaries*, which was the result of a systematic examination of 225 documentary programs broadcast by WETA in Washington, D.C., during a twelve-month period in 1987–88. The report's conclusions support the criticisms of both left and right. According to the report, the programs overall "fell short of the standard of diversity by failing to give voice to excluded groups," but they also demonstrated that "the balance of opinion tilted consistently in a liberal direction." The report continued:

> Consider that the preponderance of opinion questioned justifications for armed conflict and nuclear development, supported the primacy of environmental concerns over human need, asserted that American society discriminates against women and minorities, upheld legal interpretations of constitutional rights ranging from gay rights to search and seizure provisions, and condemned the failings of America's allies far more frequently than its Marxist opponents, at a time when the cold war was very much alive. This set of issue positions bespeaks a liberal sensibility, if not a liberal agenda, just as one could reasonably speak of a conservative sensibility if most opinion on these programs had favored a stronger defense posture, denied charges of racial and gender discrimination, opposed gay rights and restrictions on police, regularly criticized Marxist regimes, etc.[6]

The Center for Media and Public Affairs's study was concerned only with documentaries, but what all these arguments are about in the end is editorial responsibility. Who in public television is responsible for deciding what programs are broadcast? And who is responsible for monitoring and enforcing PBS's official policy of striving for fairness in every program and for balance over the course of the entire schedule?

What is, or is not, broadcast is the decision of every local station. PBS and the CPB are not licensed to broadcast; the stations are. It is the stations that must decide if there is any part of the PBS national programming feed they do not wish to transmit—for whatever reason. In making these decisions they obviously need advance warning of problem programs from PBS. The controversy over "Tongues Untied" may have grown, in part, from PBS's failure to provide stations with an adequate justification for the inclusion of the program in the national schedule.

So far as political balance and fairness are concerned, it is normally possible in a commercial station or network to locate one person at whose desk the buck stops—the president of the news division in a large network, for instance. But PBS is not itself a producing organization, so it does not have that sort of structure. The responsibility is necessarily thrown back on the CPE (which includes a vice president for news and public affairs programming). The CPE does not have direct editorial control of any single program, but it does have the considerable powers of commissioning, funding, and continuing or discontinuing series. Some would say it is editorial power at one remove ("gatekeeping" rather than editing), but it has to suffice in public television because there is no other way of doing it. In the end, nothing can go out on the national schedule (with the major exception of live, or virtually live, programs like "The MacNeil/Lehrer NewsHour") unless it has been agreed to by the CPE. Thus, the ITVS documentaries, which are causing so much speculation in conservative circles, have no automatic right to be included in the national schedule.

REGIONAL NETWORKS

Public television has four regional networks, each of which specializes in different functions. While these networks are regionally based, individual stations do not have to be located in their regions to make use of their services.

The Eastern Educational Network (EEN) is headquartered in Boston. Out of it has developed a source of programming, the American Program Service (APS), which is second only to PBS. It offers to stations (all of them, not just those in the East) an additional source of programming which is wholly market sensitive. APS attends national and international markets, negotiates rights appropriate to public television stations, and makes available to them (at very reasonable prices) programs they cannot get on the national PBS schedule. It is also a mechanism whereby stations can sometimes pool resources in order to commission or buy high-profile programs they particularly want for fundraising purposes. "The Three Tenors," for example, came to the stations not through PBS but through APS—as does a daily series, "The Nightly Business Report." APS is a major user of the public television satellite system (second only to PBS), and it currently has about thirty-seven hundred programs under contract. It is a very important alternative, and complement, to PBS.

The Southern Educational Communications Association (SECA) in Columbia, South Carolina, bears the enormous burden of running the National Instructional Television Satellite (NISS) as well as a wealth of regional projects. The Central Educational Network (CEN) outside Chicago concentrates on educational services. The Pacific Mountain Network (PMN) in Colorado runs a number of innovative projects, including a collaboration with Whittle Communications; PMN also has a special brief for Pacific Rim programming.

All these regional networks regularly supply their members with services ranging from interregional video libraries to fundraising development—not to mention the continuous exchange of programs between members.

THE PRODUCERS

Public television's own statistics show that programs broadcast on the average station come from the following production sources:

Public television stations	42.1%
Independent producers	19.4
Children's Television Workshop	16.1
Foreign producers and coproducers	14.0
Other	8.4

These figures hide a lot of subtleties. The stations themselves may be the largest producers, but very few of the 351 stations contribute to the national schedule. In fiscal 1991, PBS statistics show that the most significant station producers were the following:

WNET/WETA ("The MacNeil/Lehrer NewsHour")	260	hours
WGBH, Boston	277	
WNET, New York*	242	
WETA, Washington, D.C.†	170	
MPT (Maryland Public Television)	64	
WTTW, Chicago	47	
KCET, Los Angeles	38	
WQED, Pittsburgh	30	
KTCA, Minneapolis–St. Paul	20	
WHYY, Philadelphia	18	
KQED, San Francisco	18	

* Excluding "The MacNeil/Lehrer NewsHour"
† Including 80 hours of relays of debates and hearings from Congress but excluding "The MacNeil/Lehrer NewsHour"

Another thirty-five stations contributed between fourteen hours and thirty minutes. What this means is that three hundred stations are contributing no programs at all to the national schedule.

Everyone in public television would agree that the system is overdependent (and has always been overdependent) on a very few stations, but so great are the risks of national production that few other stations have the desire or the means to get involved. KCET in Los Angeles, now happily restored, is an example of the devastating troubles a station can get into if it overextends itself for national productions.

The statistics show that only 14 percent of production is foreign. That, too, is a subtly misleading figure. Many more programs are foreign-made but are skillfully (and very expensively) adapted to look and sound like PBS programming: many editions of "Nature," for example, and occasional editions of "Nova." Moreover, it is estimated that about one-third of public television's national programming is financed in part from overseas. Given the cost of quality programming, no one involved in television can be surprised at that figure.

Independent producers' share of the pie appears to be growing appreciably, especially since the establishment of ITVS. Most of their work is in national programming, but there are a few local outlets as well (WTTW in Chicago has broadcast "Image Union" for more than ten years as a showcase for independents). In the national schedule, independents have their own series ("P.O.V.") and contribute very largely to all sorts of other series like "The American Experience" (entirely independent), "Frontline" (80 percent), "American Playhouse" (66 percent), and "Alive from Off Center." Independents can frequently be heard demanding an even bigger share of the pie, but it has to be said that the shrillest voices are often those of the least talented. However great their initial difficulty in getting themselves noticed (and more importantly, funded), the really talented ones like Ken Burns ("The Civil War" and many other documentaries) and Henry Hampton ("Eyes on the Prize") have produced some of public television's most important and successful series.

PUBLIC TELEVISION AND THE CABLE CHANNELS

It is fashionable (particularly among those who do very little television viewing) to suggest that public television is now unnecessary because most of its programming is duplicated by cable channels, and thus can be supported by the commercial marketplace. In one of the best-remembered outbursts, one critic of public broadcasting opined that "Sesame Street" was no better than "The Flintstones" and had inspired a generation of graffiti artists.

There is no denying that cable channels have developed programming in competition with public television. Nickelodeon and Disney (children's programming), A&E and Bravo (cultural programs), the Discovery Channel and the Learning Channel (documentaries), CNN and C-SPAN (news and public affairs), and CNBC (business) are all occupying niches previously peculiar to public television. There is also no denying that all these cable channels are (or are becoming) profitable, and that most of them have acquired prestigious reputations in their own niches. It would be impossible for public television to ignore the competition that this represents.

Most people have their own opinion about the quality of television programs, but a brief survey suggests that public television retains areas of great strength. In cultural programming (both drama and music performance), "American Playhouse," "Masterpiece Theatre," and "Great Performances" have no peers (Bravo has too small an audience at the moment to be considered in the same breath as "Great Performances," "Dance in America," "Live from Lincoln Center," and "Live from the Met," while A&E appears to have moved resources away from "arts" and into other areas). In news and public affairs, "The MacNeil/Lehrer NewsHour" is unique. "Wall Street Week," "Adam Smith," "Washington Week in Review," and other weekly public affairs programs are grounded in very solid reputations; they are a part of the fabric of politics and business. Public television's children's programs are still the best—and have recently received a considerable boost. In documentaries, "Nova" and "Nature" have earned reputations equalled only by the "National Geographic Specials"— and way in advance of "Invention" or "Beyond 2000" on the Discovery Channel. "Alive from Off Center," "P.O.V.," and "Austin City Limits" cover the "flip" side. Occasional series like "Talking with David Frost," "Land of the Eagle," and Bill Moyers' programs do well by any standard. Major series—"The Civil War," "Columbus and the Age of Discovery," "Eyes on the Prize," and many more— are the icing on the cake.

It's a formidable (and very incomplete) list. How many of them might be carried on cable networks if public television were to be closed down today? Most of them; proven successes are attractive. How many of them might be developed and originated by cable networks if public television *had never existed*? Very few. Animals and David Frost (if he will pardon the conjunction) will almost always find a place on rival networks, but series like "The Civil War," while they look immensely attractive in the light of their brilliant success, were singularly unappetizing five years earlier when they were just an idea on paper with horrendous-looking budgets attached. Nor is it likely that cable channels will venture sums like $11.3 million for "Frontline," $7.8 million for "American Playhouse," and $6.9 million for "Great Performances"—the sums that PBS alone is committing to these series in 1993 (the remainder of their budgets to be made up from corporate underwriting, coproductions, and other sources).

Moreover, public television provides not just some of these programs, but all of them. That is why over five million people write checks averaging $50 to their local stations each year. That is why public television is thought of by a lot of people as a genuine network, just like the other four, with a nationwide reach and a very particular character. And all this is based on consideration of prime-time programming alone—without paying heed to public television's enormous commitment to education, which cable networks have imitated only in a small way.

Maintaining what it already has will not be good enough for public television in the next few years. As they have moved into profit, so cable channels have begun to increase their program budgets in leaps and bounds. A 1990 survey of selected cable channels by *Cablevision* showed that A&E was averaging between eight and ten minutes commercial time per hour; the Disney Channel, nine minutes; and the Learning Channel, twelve minutes. Cable budgets are still substantially smaller than public television's, but taken together (and that is the way public television has to take them) they are spending spectacularly more than public television. The Boston Consulting Group looked at four cable channels in 1990—Disney, Discovery, A&E, and CNN—and found that together they were spending $358 million on programs, compared to public television's $261 million. Each of these cable channels has increased its budget since then. Public television has not kept pace.

◆ ◆ ◆ ◆

In the next few years, competition will increase and the cost of production will rise. Public television depends so heavily on its national schedule for its prestige and income that it is unthinkable that it could allow it to deteriorate for lack of resources. The question is: Where will those resources come from? Some of them, quite clearly, could be provided by a redeployment of resources already within the system. That is mainly up to the stations, but do they have the will to do it?

And if they do have the will, what criteria will they require PBS to adopt? Quality and excellence have always been the watchwords of national programming, and they must remain so or the system will perish. But are they any longer sufficient unto themselves? There are many people within the system who believe that visibility is becoming almost as important. In an environment in which public television was generally one among only ten or twenty stations available to viewers, a single channel was sufficient. But public broadcasters now have to look forward to an environment in which the vast majority of homes will be receiving between two hundred and five hundred channels. If public television is to remain a real and visible force in the community (so the argument runs), should not every community have two, three, even four public television channels, each separately and differently scheduled?

Reinforcing the present system is the first and urgent priority, but its future needs must be assessed at the same time.

CHAPTER FIVE

DOLLARS AND CENTS:
WHERE THEY COME FROM AND WHERE THEY GO

During the 1980s public television's income virtually doubled, rising from $626 million in 1981 to about $1.25 billion in 1990. No one imagines that this sort of growth can be sustained in the 1990s. Early indications (which are admittedly against a background of recession) suggest that 1990 may even turn out to have been a plateau—in real terms, at least.

In any $1.25 billion industry there must be ways of redeploying resources. Clearly, there is some scope for that in public television, but it is much easier to do on paper than in reality. A feeling of "entitlement" is rampant within the system, and the amount of redeployment that is practicable is very different from the amount that might be desirable. There are 351 local stations to be accommodated, and they (or their 175 licensees who receive Community Service Grants from the CPB each year) effectively hold most of the purse strings.

Two areas of activity are in urgent need of extra funds: education and national programming. Incremental increases would keep them going, but more than that is necessary if they are to realize their potential—if they are to respond to technological developments and compete effectively with cable networks. So where can revenue increases come from? And why should they come?

The doubling of revenues in the 1980s was not presented to public broadcasters on a plate. They worked hard to get it. Easily the most spectacular increase came from the private sector, which rose from 41 percent of the whole in 1981 to 53.4 percent in 1990. And the biggest increases within the private sector came from subscriptions and corporate funding, both of which are forms of funding the broadcasters themselves have to solicit.

Greater funding from the private sector is a healthy trend, but main-taining it depends almost entirely on the quality and popularity of the nation-al schedule. Both individual subscribers and corporate underwriters make their contributions (which together amount to almost 40 percent of the whole budget) because of their attachment to, or their wish to be associated with, pro-grams in the national schedule. It is not instructional programming or local programming that attracts the bulk of this money. It is "Sesame Street" and "Nova," "Mystery," and "Millennium," "Frontline," and the "NewsHour." If the quality of the national schedule deteriorates—or if the programming it produces is not to the taste of corporations and subscribers—the results will be catastrophic.

At the moment the national schedule accounts for approximately 21 per-cent of total spending by public television, and the amount spent on it (about $260 million) has remained virtually flat for the past three years.*

Public television's tax-based income comes from state governments (19.3 percent), the federal government (16.2 percent), state colleges and universities (6.6 percent), and local governments (3.7 percent). For all of them, education is public television's principal (but not sole) purpose. And for all of them, times are hard.

A state-by-state comparison reveals startling differences in the levels of state contributions—ranging in 1990 from New York's $27.2 million to Wyoming's $19.00 (sic). The fairest way to codify it is by looking at the con-tributions of states (including both state governments and state colleges and uni-versities, which will help to get Wyoming out of the doghouse) on a per capita basis. Figures for 1990[1] show that the leaders in the field were the following:

1.	Vermont	$6.50
2.	Alaska	6.30
3.	South Carolina	6.15
4.	Nebraska	5.68
5.	South Dakota	4.07

The bottom of the table tells a different story:

43.	Wyoming	$0.25
44.	Massachusetts	0.21
	Missouri	0.21
46.	Texas	0.15
47.	California	0.12
48.	Colorado	0.10
	Nevada	0.10

(Delaware has no public television station)

---

* Final figures for FY 1992 show a 13.7% increase to $300 million.

Subsequent years have seen budget cuts in almost every state. New York's contribution, for instance, was cut by $8 million (almost one-third) in 1991. Nevertheless, the moral is clear: Some states put considerable resources into public television, others do not. And no government in the 1990s—be it federal, state, or local—is likely to increase its funding unless a very strong case is made—a mission defined. The responsibility for doing that rests squarely with the local stations. They will be assisted by PBS, American Public Television Stations (the lobbying and advocacy organization in Washington), and the CPB, but it is the stations that must convince their local authorities and representatives of the urgency of the case.

SOURCES OF INCOME

The data from fiscal 1990, the latest year for which figures were readily available at the time of writing, show the breakdown of public television's revenues (Table 5.1).

TABLE 5.1
PUBLIC TELEVISION'S SOURCES OF INCOME, FISCAL YEAR 1990

Source	$ million	% of total
Corporation for Public Broadcasting	168.6	13.5 (Federal)
Grants and contracts	33.8	2.7 (Federal)
Local governments	46.1	3.7
State governments	241.1	19.3
State colleges/universities	81.8	6.6
Other public colleges/universities	9.9	0.8
Private colleges/universities	19.5	1.6
Foundations	57.7	4.6
Business (incl. corporate underwriting)	209.8	16.8
Subscribers/memberships	273.3	21.9
Auctions	21.5	1.7
Other	85.0	6.8
Total Income:	1,248.1	
Total federal income	202.4	16.2
Total nonfederal income	1,045.7	83.8
Tax-based income	583.4	46.7
Private sector income	664.8	53.3

Source: CPB Planning and Analysis, November 1991.

EXPENDITURE

The way public television spent its money in fiscal 1990, shown in Table 5.2, is taken from statistics supplied by PBS. The total expenditure is greater than the total income detailed in the previous table because program expenditures frequently cross over financial years, with monies voted in one year not actually being spent until the next.

TABLE 5.2
PUBLIC TELEVISION EXPENDITURES, FISCAL YEAR 1990

	$ million	% of Total
Programming: total expenditures	615.3	48.8
National (including PBS General Assessment) 280.6		
Regional (estimated) 30.8		
Local production and acquisition 303.9		
Technical	202.3	16.0
Management	198.9	15.8
Fundraising	141.8	11.2
Underwriting	70.5	5.6
Public Information	16.7	1.3
Depreciation	16.4	1.3
Total Expenditure	1,261.9	100

Source: PBS Economic Analysis, March 1992.

In 1990, the Corporation for Public Broadcasting commissioned a study by the Boston Consulting Group (BCG). The study—Strategies for Public Television in a Multi-Channel Environment (March 1991)—made a number of provocative and controversial recommendations, most of which followed logically from BCG's analysis of public television's spending and revenues and the relationship between them. Expenditures, for instance, were broken down in more revealing ways than the PBS analysis reproduced above, and revenues were looked at in terms of what generated them rather than who donated them. The correlations are shown in Table 5.3 (figures are for 1989).

TABLE 5.3

BCG ANALYSIS OF PUBLIC TELEVISION'S EXPENDITURES AND REVENUES FOR 1989

	Cost $ million	Generated $ million
National programming (incl. all overheads and associated costs, e.g., local station administrative costs)	390	660
Instructional programming	60	180
Local production (incl. program personnel and studio costs, on-air fundraising costs, and outreach activities)	470	210
Local distribution (signal and "last mile" costs)	170	180
Local rescheduling (including purchasing and administrative costs)	100	100

Source: The Boston Consulting Group, Strategies for Public Television in a Multi-Channel Environment, March 1990.

Whether or not they accept the BCG's methodology or the precise figures, most people agree with its conclusion: National programming and instructional programming both generate revenue, whereas local production costs a great deal more than it generates. Most people also agree with the first part of BCG's recommendation:

> The goal of the national and instructional programming should be to compete against commercial networks through superior quality. Resources should be substantially increased to enable this on the order of $250 million in new funds by the end of the decade. . . .

But they absolutely do not agree on the next part of the BCG's recommendation:

> It is unlikely that new revenues can make up more than a fraction of what is needed. The major contribution should be expected to come at the expense of those local production activities that consume resources out of proportion to the revenues that they generate or their value to viewers or to society.

There is no suggestion in the BCG study that public television's "bedrock of localism" should be changed or weakened; if anything, it should be solidified, but (the BCG argues) this must involve a redefinition of the local station's role and functions. This is the most fundamental strategic argument within public television today. It is explored in more detail in Chapters Four and Six.

The BCG report was distributed to all the local stations. That may be the end of the matter—but probably not, because the BCG's findings were, at the very least, a warning to the stations. The wise ones have taken notice.

THE NATIONAL PROGRAMMING BUDGET

Increased spending on national programming is mandated not just by inflation but by the competitive environment in which public television finds itself. Niche cable services (such as A&E, The Discovery Channel, and Nickelodeon) are centralized operations with much lower overhead and production costs than public television. Moreover, they are finding their niches profitable and are therefore able to increase their program budgets spectacularly. Paul Kagan Associates reports the following actual and projected expenditures on programs:

TABLE 5.4

PROGRAM EXPENDITURES (ACTUAL AND PROJECTED $ MILLION)

	1990	1991	1992
Nickelodeon	54.0	67.0	77.0
Arts & Entertainment	38.4	50.6	57.2
The Discovery Channel	38.0	52.0	75.0
The Learning Channel	3.5	6.4	8.5

Source: Paul Kagan Associates—quoted in *PBS Economic Analysis,* March 1992.

These numbers do not look very large when compared to public television's national programming budget of approximately $262 million, but it is the aggregate budget of all the competing channels (not just the ones quoted above) with which public television has to be concerned. The cable networks do very little production of their own; mainly, they are in the more economic business of acquisition. And while their program budgets are rising steeply, public television's has been more or less static since 1989:

1989	$261.9 million
1990	$258.4 million
1991	$262.8 million

The core of the national programming budget is the sum of money now held by the Chief Program Executive at PBS. It is in excess of $100 million a year; it is pledged two years in advance (so that it can genuinely be used as the "critical mass" around which other monies can be coalesced); and it comes mainly (about 75 percent) from the stations, in the form of a levy, with the CPB making up the balance by the automatic donation of half its Program Fund.

Important as that core is, the following estimates for 1991 national programming (Table 5.4) show that, while both the stations and the CPB kicked in some extra funds later in the process, their combined contributions represent less than half the whole.

TABLE 5.5

CONTRIBUTORS TO PBS NATIONAL PROGRAM FUNDING, FISCAL YEAR 1991

	$ million	% of total
Public television stations	89.2	34.1
Corporation for Public Broadcasting	37.5	14.3
Business/corporations	73.0	28.1
Foundations	23.9	9.0
Government (NEA, NEH, NSF, etc.)	12.0	4.4
Private producers	20.8	7.6
Individuals	2.0	0.8
Associations, unions, and other	4.3	1.7

Source: PBS Economic Analysis, March 1992.

The principal "losses" to the national program budget since 1989 have been in federal grants from the National Endowment for the Arts, National Endowment for the Humanities, National Science Foundation, and other federal agencies, (down from $20.5 million to $12.0 million)* and the in-kind contributions of coproducers (down from $31 million to $20 million).† Corporate, foundation, and CPB contributions have been relatively flat. The slack has been taken up by the local stations, whose aggregate contribution to national programming has risen from $62.5 million in 1988 to $89.2 million in 1991. Many within the system think this is still a very modest contribution (it is about 7.5 percent of public television's total operating budget), and the agreed increases for 1992 and 1993 were very modest (3.1 percent and 3.6 percent respectively).

* Back up to $18.6 million in fiscal year 1992.
† Up to $47.6 million in fiscal year 1992—a spectacular 115% increase.

Nevertheless, it is not the whole picture. A few (a very few) of the larger stations, in addition to their pro rata contributions to the levy on stations, are taking the considerable risks involved in actually producing programs for the national schedule. These risks often involve the giving of completion guarantees and the necessity of committing to production when not all the money is in place. Thus (to give just one example), WNET, New York, is the producer of a major series called "Dancing," which will air in 1993. The series is a large-scale international coproduction made over a period of more than three years. For much of that time WNET was at risk for $2.5 million—until a foundation was found to bridge the gap during the final months of production. That example can be multiplied many times over by WNET, WGBH, WETA, and the few other stations capable of major production.

FEDERAL FUNDING

Federal government funding of public television has always been controversial, but it has almost always commanded the support of a bipartisan majority in Congress. The original Carnegie commission recommended that federal funding should come from the proceeds of an excise tax on the sale of television sets. Over the years, other bodies have come up with variations on the theme—*inter alia*:

- Surtaxes on residential electricity and telephone bills

- A spectrum tax

- Government matching of private contributions

- Use of part of government revenues from taxes on commercial broadcasters (without raising those taxes)

- A tax on households having a television set

- Taxes on license transfers when commercial stations are sold

- Taxes on advertising revenues of commercial broadcasters or cable operators, or both

None of these proposals has reached first base. Although government matching funds are included in current legislation they are at the rate of $1 for every $2.50 of nonfederal contributions; in fact, public television is actually raising $5.20 for every federal dollar. The nearest approach to first base was probably a 1988 attempt in the Senate Commerce Committee to create a public broadcasting trust whose funds would come from a fee (2 to 5 percent) levied on the transfer of all properties licensed by the FCC. Like all such proposals, it was unacceptable to commercial broadcasters—and would not have been very effective in periods of recession, when very few licenses change hands.

In the end, the argument has always come back to general tax revenues and the authorizing and appropriating of funds in the customary way. The problem for public television is that, unlike other organizations and agencies that draw on public funds, television needs to know its spending levels several years in advance because of the long timescales involved in program production ("The Civil War" took five years). For a brief, shining hour between 1975 and 1978, five-year authorizations and three-year appropriations were legislated (together with a matching formula), but these were taken away by the Carter administration in 1978. Since then, it has always been three-year authorizations and (effectively) two-year appropriations—except when the system has broken down completely, as in 1982–84. Even when the system works, it is not entirely reliable: in 1990 the administration withdrew $96.8 million of appropriated monies three months before the beginning of the financial year; the funding was restored later.

The CPB received its first federal appropriation ($5 million) in 1969. The 1992 appropriation was just over $251 million and was shared between radio and television. In addition, Congress appropriates money each year for the Public Telecommunications Facilities Program ($22.9 million in 1992), and occasionally makes special grants, such as the $200 million it voted for satellite replacement between 1991 and 1993 (funds that almost certainly could not have been found elsewhere). Measured in constant dollars, (based on the Bureau of Labor Statistics' Consumer Price Index), the value of the CPB appropriation more than doubled in the 1970s, but it declined by about 2 percent between 1980 and 1990 (mainly due to the reductions imposed by the Reagan administration in 1983).

The legislation recently passed by the Senate should give public broadcasting substantial increases in federal funding for the years 1994–96. They are compared with the 1993 figure, which was authorized under the previous (1988) legislation:

1993	$285 million (excluding satellite replacement)
1994	$310 million
1995	$375 million
1996	$425 million

These authorizations are for television *and* radio. What's more, they are only authorizations (or ceilings). The actual appropriation for 1993 is $253.31 million—well short of the $285 million originally authorized.

Regardless of whether it is relevant or appropriate, it is interesting to compare our federal funding of public broadcasting with that of other countries. CPB figures for 1992 show that we are spending approximately $1.06 per head of population. Japan spends $17.71 per head for NHK, Canada spends $32.15 per head for the CBC, and the United Kingdom spends $38.56 for the BBC.

While most people agree that our system of authorizations is the most practicable one available, it is nevertheless tempting (for the future) to return to the search for a dedicated tax from which to fund the federal government's contributions. Any system that would produce more reliable and long-term funding would be a step forward for public broadcasting. For instance, it cannot pass notice that a number of large telecommunications organizations are currently seeking regulatory relief in order to enter new businesses. The telephone companies want changes in the Modified Final Judgment of 1982 (the breakup of Ma Bell) in order to enter the lucrative business of supplying video services to homes on fiber-optic systems. At the same time, cable operators are looking for relief from cross-ownership restrictions that ban them from owning other businesses (like television stations) in markets where they already own a cable system. Supposing either, or both, of these groups were to get the franchises they covet, might they not pay a franchise fee, a portion of which could go to finance public broadcasting?

Or there is the possibility of a spectrum user fee (espoused by the second Carnegie commission as long ago as 1978). In the words of former PBS president Larry Grossman: "Broadcasting is the only industry in America where you can make money off a public resource and not pay a thing for it. If you drill for oil on public land, you pay a fee. If your cattle graze on public land, you pay a fee." So why shouldn't broadcasters pay a fee, too? A spectrum user fee of, say, 2 percent would gross an estimated $1 billion a year. If some of this were to be earmarked for public broadcasting it would provide the funding stability so urgently needed for the system—and as a *quid pro quo*, Grossman suggests, commercial broadcasters might be given some further deregulation (such as the public interest provisions, which are little regarded in any case).

There has always been a body of opinion virulently opposed to the whole idea of federal funding for public television. Recent debates, both in the Senate and in the press, have suggested that this body of opinion has grown, and is growing. It comes almost exclusively from the conservative side of the political spectrum. In January 1992 the Heritage Foundation published *Making Public Television Public*. This paper advocated "selling the CPB to the private sector, allowing it to operate as a publicly held corporation accountable to its shareholders."[2] Leaving aside the fact that the CPB (whose only assets are its annual appropriations from Congress) is hardly salable, the argument is that public television should be privatized—made to go commercial. Among the reasons deduced are the following :

- Public television is insufficiently accountable.

- Cable channels already cover most of the areas of programming scheduled on public television.

- Public television's programs lack objectivity and balance, and display a liberal bias.

- Certain organizations and individuals financed in part by the public money appropriated to public television are making large profits for themselves.

- Public television's "enhanced underwriting" guidelines are robbing commercial television of advertising.

- In Great Britain (Channel 4), France (TF1), and other countries, ventures similar to public television have been successfully established (or adapted) as commercial rather than state-funded organizations.

Critics of federal funding—even those not committed to killing it altogether—may wonder why it is so important to public television. After all, it accounts for only 16 percent of total revenues.

Anyone who has been involved in fundraising of any sort appreciates the importance of the very first contribution, especially when it comes from a weighty and prestigious source. However small it may be as a percentage of the target, there is a sense in which it is the "critical mass." This is certainly the case for public television; federal funding, particularly when it is authorized well in advance, provides the system with its continuity and its permanence. It is the base from which PBS and the stations are able to go out and not just double it, but quintuple it at least.

CORPORATE UNDERWRITING

Corporate support accounts for about 17 percent of public television's total budget and about 28 percent ($73 million*) of the national programming budget. As a percentage of total U.S. television advertising expenditures (which are well over $20 billion a year) it is a fleabite, but a very important fleabite for public television.

Ever since 1976 PBS has promulgated, and occasionally revised, *Standards and Practices for National Program Funding*. They are based on three principles:

- PBS will not allow editorial control to be exercised by program funders.

---

* In fiscal year 1992, it increased to $89.5 million, a 22 percent increase.

- PBS must guard against the public perception that editorial control might have been exercised by program funders.

- Public television must vigorously protect its noncommercial character.

While there is no intention, and no possibility, of the first two of these principles being intentionally diluted, it is frequently argued that public television could make some compromises on the third principle and thereby increase its revenues. Did not the introduction of "enhanced underwriting" in 1984 produce an immediate increase of more than 30 percent in underwriting income? And, despite enhanced underwriting, isn't it true that only 1.7 percent of public television's total air time is given over to underwriting credits, in contrast to the nearly 17 percent of air time commercial networks give to advertising?

There is very little evidence that the liberalizing of underwriting guidelines would automatically lead to any increase in corporate support— not, at any rate, without a move from underwriting to advertising and the consequent surrender of public television's most distinctive quality: uninterrupted programs of excellence. Many people argue that public television has already gone far enough down that road. Some believe it has gone too far.

As far as on-air credits are concerned, PBS issues the following guidelines[3] to corporations and other funders of national programs:

> On-air credits are usually introduced by a statement such as "funding for this program has been made possible by [your company's name]." Beyond the introductory statement, you may:

> - describe the business you are in, mentioning up to four target markets, product lines or services;

> - use a fully animated treatment of your company's logo, a musical signature, and, in most cases, your slogan;

> - show one specific product, or symbolically depict up to four product types or product lines;

> - show employees of your company as an alternative to product description; and

> - use images from the program as background for the identification of your company.

> Your credit may be up to fifteen seconds long, depending on the funding level, the number of underwriters, and other factors.

In no case, even when a program has three or more underwriters, can the length of opening and closing credits exceed thirty seconds. Only when a program runs longer than seventy-five minutes can it be interrupted (by an intermission during an opera or ballet, for instance) to allow the underwriter to receive more than just the statutory opening and closing credits. And the guidelines require that there can be no product brand identification in credits on programs targeted primarily at children under twelve years of age.

These are guidelines that must be observed on national programs distributed by PBS. But local stations also have the right (and the need) to take on local underwriters. Not all stations observe such rigid guidelines on their own air as they are bound to observe for national programming. Nevertheless, it is perfectly possible for a station, while properly observing the PBS guidelines for national programs, to have a much more commercial "look" than is normally associated with public broadcasting. One of the most successful public stations, WTTW, Chicago, is often cited as an example. In fact, when you look closely at WTTW you find less crediting clutter than on most other stations, but there is no doubt that you also find a very high degree of on-air professionalism. To the extent that that is "commercial," WTTW would probably be happy to plead guilty. Other stations, such as WNET, New York, approach much closer to the borderline by showing what are called General Support Announcements (GSAs), which may often be paid announcements by nonprofit organizations (both Ireland and the Bahamas promote tourism in this way). But the most common (and potentially the most dangerous) practice among stations is to allow national programs (replete with credits for funders, some of whom may have contributed millions of dollars) to be preceded by credits for local sponsors that have contributed very small amounts to cover just the local transmission costs of the station. Since 1987 PBS has made this practice more difficult by designating some national programs that are underwritten by a single corporation or foundation "exclusive." In other cases there is a real danger that valuable national funding may be jeopardized by local practices. PBS would prefer that stations take on what are called "daypart" underwriters—corporations that can properly be credited for underwriting all or part of a day's transmission on that particular station.

Advertising agencies are generally derisive of the skills of public broadcasters in making pitches to them. They compare them unfavorably with cable channels. The truth is that advertising agencies have very little interest in urging their clients to underwrite programs on public television; there is little or no profit for the agency in such a transaction. But the stations are undoubtedly putting much more vigor into their marketing efforts, putting together packages of off-air, rather than on-air, benefits for underwriters. This is frequently a way in which corporations can gain legitimate attention in the most difficult market of all—the educational market. It is also a way in which they can target very specific subsections of the population, from children to opera-goers. A combination of the prestige to be gained from on-air credits associated with a successful, high-quality series, plus a package of off-air benefits, plus a further investment in tune-in advertising, can often help a corporation implement marketing strategies at a reasonable cost—not, perhaps, to be measured in CPMs (cost-per-thousands), but much more often in terms of demographic targeting.

There seems to be no reason why corporate underwriting should diminish in the future. It is probable, however, that most underwriting will take the form of medium- and small-sized contributions. Grants in the range of $250,000 or $500,000 will be much more likely than blockbuster grants of $3 million or more—which is all right for most series. But there are some—"The MacNeil/Lehrer NewsHour" is an obvious example—that can probably survive only with the sort of blockbuster grants they have come to rely on; the alternative would have to be massively increased contributions from the CPE, which is even more unlikely.

There are two important provisos for corporate underwriting. The first is that public television must retain its uncommercial, uncluttered look. In all probability, that is what the members—the individual subscribers—require; even a fairly substantial increase in corporate underwriting would not offset a downturn in individual giving. The second proviso is that the national schedule has to continue to attract corporate money by the nature of its programming. Corporations will not want to be associated with controversial programming; they are much more likely to back the conservative than the radical. That is the nature of the beast. It is a fine line for programmers to tread, and it will be one of the litmus tests by which the new Chief Program Executive experiment will be judged, for corporate money represents almost 30 percent of the budget for national programming.

LOCAL STATIONS AND FUNDRAISING

It is estimated that roughly 5.1 million people subscribed $280.7 million to public television in 1991, an average contribution of $55.04. The number of subscribers had doubled since 1980, and the average contribution had risen from less than $30.

All this represents local effort. There is no other place in public television to which the individual citizen can subscribe, other than to his or her local station. And the stations possess the most potent and effective tool yet devised for mass fundraising—television air time. Most stations make use of three designated "pledge weeks" in the year (one each in March, August, and December) for which additional funding is available from the Station Independence Program for the acquisition and commissioning of special programs. Some stations find it unnecessary to use all three weeks, fearful of an audience reaction against too much "begging." A few stations (about eighty-two at the last count) still hold on-air auctions, for which PBS's National Auction Service gives them assistance by obtaining highly marketable donated goods.

The reported income from these activities is, of course, gross income. It is impossible to estimate what the true figure—the net income—might be, simply because the expenses of the fundraising operation vary wildly from station to station. For some, it is the principal *raison d'être*: all their resources and facilities exist for that purpose. For others, it is a small (but very important) part of their overall effort.

Fundraising is a sophisticated activity. It requires professional people, professionally trained. It also requires station managers and board members to be intimately involved in the process and totally committed to it. And it requires a long-term strategy—a strategy that will place less reliance on thrice-yearly solicitations on the screen, and more on development of multiyear (even lifetime) support within the community. There is a danger—a real one—that the appeal of public television's uncluttered, uninterrupted programming may be undone by the too frequent use of the pledge-week formula (especially, as is far too frequently the case, when it is badly and amateurishly done).

According to the Nielsen Television Index, approximately eighty-seven million Americans watch public television sometime each week. About 6 percent of them respond to the stations' membership drives. In itself, that is not a bad percentage, but there is little sign that individual membership is being increased incrementally from year to year. Nor is there a great deal of ambition in the development strategies of many of the stations: only 40 out of the 345 stations have established major gift programs to entice annual gifts of $1,000 or more.

Even fewer stations have established endowments. The reason is unclear. If a station sees itself as a genuine community resource, especially an educational resource like a university or library, then shouldn't it be able to establish an endowment, just as they do? Stations that have done it rejoice in the benefits. Oklahoma ETA, for instance, has an annual income of $600,000 from its endowment established in the early 1980s, and that is doubtless one reason why it is able to concentrate its on-air fundraising into one sixteen-day "festival" in March each year (uniquely, a "viewer-driven" festival made up of programs voted for by viewers in a ballot: it brings in nearly $2.5 million).

Two things stand out in a survey of station fundraising: (1) too much of it takes place on-screen, and (2) it is almost wholly dependent on the appeal of the national schedule. It is tempting to think that by subtly changing the nature of the national schedule it would be possible to increase the audience. But, for public television, increasing the audience does not necessarily mean increasing the revenue. It is possible to increase the audience with nonsubscribers while at the same time driving away some traditional subscribers.

In 1981 Congress amended the Telecommunications Act to allow public television to increase its income by earning money: "Each public broadcasting station shall be authorized to engage in the offering of services, facilities or products in exchange for remuneration."

Thus, stations are able to rent out excess studio space; accept advertising in their program guides; and sell books, transcripts, and teacher guides based on public television programming. PBS can lease spare time on its satellite transponders and earn income for itself and the stations by exploiting the technology it has itself developed. PBS Enterprises, for instance, is a wholly owned for-profit subsidiary that develops goods and services in areas of new technology. Through its subsidiary, National Datacast, PBS Enterprises is exploiting one of the PBS engineers' latest breakthroughs, the use of an unused portion of the television signal (the so-called Vertical Blanking Interval) for transmitting high-speed data. As yet, these ventures have not produced a lot of money; PBS Enterprises projected gross revenues of $1 million in 1992.

PBS Video, on the other hand, is an in-house division that distributes video cassettes of public television programs in the nontheatric market (schools, colleges, libraries, hospitals, government agencies, and so on). Its 1991 sales amounted to $8.2 million. After fulfillment and payment of royalties, PBS nets a small percentage of that figure.

But the real purpose of entrepreneurial ventures like these is not to make money for PBS. Ideally, they should be designed to enable *the stations* to make money. Thus, PBS has created its own home video label—PBS Home Video—and it has licensed Pacific Arts as the exclusive distributor of that label, on condition that all public television stations are allowed to purchase tapes at 52 percent off retail. A similar scheme established by WGBH in Boston—PBS Public Video Service—enables member stations to use their own marketing capacities (both on the screen through 800 numbers and in mailings to their members) to sell tapes at fairly considerable profit. In an initial pilot scheme in the summer of 1991, PBS Public Video Service, working with the wholesaler Commtrom and about twenty stations, tested an on-air home video offer of "I, Claudius" that resulted in thirty-five hundred sales. Meanwhile, PBS Home Video (whose titles include "The Civil War") made sales totaling more than $30 million in a fourteen month period in 1991–92.

WGBH may be the most entrepreneurial station in the system; it certainly has the most to be entrepreneurial about. In addition to PBS Public Video Service, WGBH has a joint venture with Minnesota Public Radio in the *Signals* mail-order catalog and its own shop in Boston (soon to be increased to three shops). Even so, its income from all these activities amounts to no more than 4 percent to 5 percent of its operating budget.

Although it is no more than a gleam in the eye at the moment, WGBH, along with PBS and WNET, is developing the idea of a pay cable channel. A feasibility study is under way. The idea harks back to a proposal first made ten years ago in a study funded by the Carnegie Corporation—*Keeping PACE with the New Television*—which recommended the establishment of a national nonprofit pay cable television network for the performing arts, culture, and education (PACE). At the time, it failed to win favor with either the Congress or public broadcasters, but perhaps its day has now come.

There are two principal, or potential, barriers to the expansion of money-making activities in public television. The first is the tax laws. Like all other nonprofits, stations must pay tax on "unrelated business income," defined as income derived from activities that do not "contribute importantly" to the achievement of a station's original purposes. But on the sale of print materials that complement public television programs, or on the sale of advertising space in program guides, stations do not pay tax (and for this reason they go to great lengths to ensure that these activities are not in any way subsidized by federal funds). However, the ruling that exempts these revenues from taxation is under attack from a coalition of for-profit businesses. Any change in the law could adversely affect public television's incentive to earn extra income.

More important is the fact that public television's business is programs— but to make money from the sale and distribution of programs in the national and international markets you must first own the necessary rights. Quality programs are very expensive to produce. More and more, it is necessary to bring in coproducers—in effect, to give away certain rights in exchange for the up-front financing needed to make the programs. To do otherwise will require considerably more funding than public television has at its disposal for such productions. Certainly, if it owned outright the worldwide television rights and the worldwide video rights (instead of just the PBS television rights) in productions like "Great Performances" or "Nature," there would be profits to be made. But it is difficult to see how such rights could be regularly acquired without access to a substantial pool of additional funding.

◆   ◆   ◆   ◆

Is public television poor? Is it underfunded? As always, the answers depend on one's viewpoint. National programming is certainly underfunded at the moment and will become more so as competition from cable channels increases and production costs begin to escalate (as they normally do in a postrecession climate). It is equally clear that the whole educational effort of public television needs to retool and expand its methods of dissemination. That will cost money.

Look at it another way: Public television's operating budget of $1.2 billion represents only 4.5 percent of the total revenues available to commercial television in this country.

Yet another way to look at it is to compare public television's budget with those of other countries. CPB statistics (August 1991) show public television's budget at $1.26 billion—compared to:

◆   CBC in Canada (all its television effort, including French and English Services): $988.3 million.

◆   BBC in Great Britain (television only): $1.57 billion. For that, the BBC runs two full national networks, competing in the sports and entertainment fields as well as the informational and educational; it has regional networks and production centers in Wales, Scotland, and Northern Ireland (as well as five in England); and it is the actual producer of the vast majority of all the programs it transmits.

In a way, both the CBC and the BBC are false comparisons because neither of them has the basis in localism that is the principal characteristic of the American system.

Many observers conclude that while public television in this country clearly needs additional funding for specific purposes—namely, educational and national programming—there is also a considerable amount of money in the system that needs to be looked at closely to see just how effectively it is being allocated. This is the $570 million that is spent each year on local production and local station operations. It is not helpful to look at it just in terms of cost effectiveness; a better yardstick might be "mission effectiveness." How much are the stations contributing to the system? And how much are they weighing it down?

Chapter Six

WEIGHTS AND MEASURES

It is widely believed that public television's financial problems are secondary to its organizational problems. Almost everyone who has ever worked in public television, or dealt with it, has complained about its bureaucracy and its difficulty in making decisions. But the facts don't really support this picture. The bureaucracy is not as large as it is often made out to be. About 350 people work at PBS in Alexandria, Virginia, and just over 200 at the CPB in Washington. There are, of course, examples of bureaucracy getting in the way. The Program Challenge Fund, which is jointly administered by PBS and the CPB, is a good example: in order to get a challenge grant, not only must producers satisfy both the Chief Program Executive at PBS and the Director of the Program Fund at the CPB, they must also have separate contracts with each of them.

In the end, it is not bureaucracy that impedes decisionmaking in public television; it is democracy. The 351 local stations (or, at any rate, their 175 licensees) are virtually sovereign. PBS is their organization—they own it and run it. And so far as the CPB is concerned, although the stations are answerable to it for the use of their federal funding, the largest part of that funding (the annual Community Service Grants [CSGs] given by the CPB to all qualified stations) is all but automatic. In the end, the stations are the only powerful agents of change in the system. If they do not want change, there is little anyone else can do about it—except to maintain "the continuing drift of the status quo."

Three changes might make a major difference:

♦   The boosting of the National Program Service, both in the amount of its programming and in its funding

- The expansion of public television's educational broadcasting effort into new delivery systems (satellite and video technologies being the most important), with programming to match

- The adaptation of local stations to meet the requirements of these first two changes—neither of which can be fully achieved unless the role and function of the local public television station is substantially revised and expanded

All this is dictated by overarching changes in the U.S. media environment—in technology, in education, in the competitive environment in which public television finds itself. In these circumstances the principal engine of change ought to be fear—fear of becoming irrelevant.

It is a fact (and an oft-quoted one in the recent Senate debates) that in this $1.25 billion industry only $500 million is spent on programs and over $700 million on administration and overhead. It is a fact that national and instructional programming, both of them starved for funds, generate almost all the income. It is a fact that local programming consumes nearly half the system's total resources for only 7 percent of its air time.

Against these facts one must set the enormous advantages of localism—the presence in almost every community that enables public television to have access to its largest single source of revenue: the American people. It is hard to see how public television can advance into its second quarter-century with a reasonable certainty of expanding its role and its importance, without its continuing basis in localism.

◆ ◆ ◆ ◆

The downside of localism is clearly expressed in the statistics, but cost effectiveness is not, in itself, a sufficient measurement of local stations' contributions. "Mission effectiveness" is a fairer yardstick. How well do they serve their communities? And in doing so, how well do they serve public television in general?

There are undoubtedly a number of outstanding stations and statewide systems. There are stations with exceptional local programming, like those in Phoenix and Chicago; there are state systems with long-standing and impressive commitments to education, like those in South Carolina, Kentucky, and Nebraska; there are stations pursuing highly distinctive local missions, like those in Detroit and Pittsburgh; there are model, forward-looking stations like the one in Seattle, and highly effective state university stations like the one at University Park, Pennsylvania; there are individual states pouring resources into state-of-the-art systems, like Iowa, Oregon, and South Dakota; and there are the great producing stations in Boston, New York, and Washington without which national programming would be almost nonexistent. These are just random examples.

But one cannot escape the statistics of the system as a whole. There is no such thing, in reality, as an average station, yet it is possible to construct a profile of a *statistically* average station from the mass of research in the Boston Consulting Group study. According to these statistics, the "average" station broadcasts 5,903 hours per year.

TABLE 6.1

PROFILE OF AN "AVERAGE" STATION

Source	hours per annum	% of hours	cost $ thousands	% of budget
PBS programming	3,848	64	500	24
Local acquisition	1,950	34	150	7
Local production	105	2	1,500	69

The station's entire overhead is, of course, contained in the final line—and the local production cost includes not just on-air programming but any outreach and community activities the station may be involved in. The average amount of money raised from individual subscribers by that "average" station is about $800,000.

The size of overheads is clearly one problem. The CPB's Equal Employment Opportunity Report for 1991 shows 11,215 people being employed full-time by the 351 stations—certainly not an outrageous figure. But the biggest contributor to the overhead is the cost of the stations' facilities and hardware; even if they are used only to conduct fundraising programs, a station must still lease or own a studio and broadcasting equipment. Even in the big production centers there is cause to wonder at overheads. The biggest individual operating budget in the system is that of WNET, New York— currently about $120 million. By way of comparison, CNN's total operating budget of $312 million allows it to deliver CNN, CNN International (including twenty-eight overseas bureaus), and Headline News—each of them twenty-four hours a day.

Another problem is the number of stations. The three big commercial networks—ABC, CBS, and NBC—each have between 209 and 220 local stations (including both owned-and-operateds and affiliates) with which they each cover 99 percent of the nation. Public television has 351 stations, which gives it 98 percent coverage. As a comparison, that is somewhat misleading, since public television stations have altogether different missions than commercial stations, and some (university and college stations, for instance) have highly specialized missions. Nevertheless, there is a major problem of overlapping. The CPB estimates that 111 of the 351 stations overlap one another in some way. Many of these overlaps are unavoidable. Sometimes there are major metropolitan areas in close proximity (Washington, D.C., and Baltimore; Waco and Dallas; Chicago and Gary). Sometimes there are metropolitan areas close to state boundaries (Omaha, Sioux City, Charlotte).

But there are also large metropolitan areas in which there are multiple licensees: The New York area has seven, the Bay Area five, and Los Angeles four. In some of these there is strong antipathy between certain stations (WNET and WLIW in New York, KQED and KTEH in the Bay Area), but there are also stations with distinctively different missions (WNYC and WNYE in New York; KLCS in Los Angeles; and KMPT, which is minority-controlled, in San Francisco). Another group of cities—perhaps ten of them, including Boston, Minneapolis-St. Paul, and Pittsburgh—have two stations owned by a single licensee; here one assumes there should be no duplication of schedules. There are also magnificently inexplicable overlaps: the 202nd market in the country, Bowling Green, Kentucky, has two public television licensees! In summary:

- 17 percent of the nation has access to four or more public television channels

- 11 percent has access to three channels

- 30 percent has access to two channels

- 36 percent has access to only one channel

There is a twofold problem in these overlaps. On the one hand, they force stations to compete with one another for members and subscriptions within the same area. On the other hand, some of the stations duplicate one another's program schedules. Although it is rare for overlapping stations to broadcast the same programs simultaneously, a significant number broadcast the same basic programming at different times.

There is, however, an argument in favor of overlapping. In the not-so-distant future most of the country's major urban and suburban areas (and some rural areas as well) will be served by cable systems offering 200 or more different channels. In order to retain visibility on these systems (the argument runs) public television will need more than one channel—preferably several. The 1992 Cable Consumer Protection Act, specifically foresees this situation and directs that "all cable operators shall continue to provide carriage to all qualified local noncommercial educational television stations whose signals were carried on their systems as of March 29, 1990." It even goes so far as to direct that any cable system whose franchise area does not include a public television station must import the signal of one from a neighboring area. As far as new stations—those established after March 29, 1990—are concerned, cable systems are bound to carry them unless their programming "substantially duplicates" the programming of a station already being carried.

If overlapping stations are to be able to develop nonduplicating schedules, they will need more programming from which to choose. One solution might be for PBS to carry not just two, but several, different services on its satellite feeds; the new Telstar 401 satellite transponders that will come into operation in December 1993 will give it the technical capacity to do that. PBS already sends out two separate feeds—one for instructional/educational programs, the other for prime-time programs. In the future, given the resources, PBS plans to create several more services—a literacy channel, a math and science channel, a college credit course channel, a General Education Development (GED) channel, an adult education channel, and others. (Not all of these channels would be for broadcast use: some would be for direct satellite transmission and others would be supplemented by video software.) There should also be programming services for minorities, to serve stations like KBDI, Denver; WHMM, Washington D.C.; KMPT, San Francisco; and other stations that hopefully will be created for that purpose. But "given the resources" is the operative phrase. In these circumstances, and with the continuing availability of relatively low-priced alternative prime-time programming from EEN's American Program Service and the other regional networks, duplication of programming within the same markets will be less excusable.

But even if they have nonduplicated schedules, overlapping stations will still be soliciting membership and subscriptions in competition with one another. The recent experience of public radio has been that the more stations there are in an area, the bigger the total amount of money they bring in from that area (provided they are each supplying a different kind of programming). That may be true of public television, too, but it does not alter the fact that each of the overlapping stations will have its own facilities and overhead to cover, as well as the cost of its programming. The net amount of income from fundraising is what matters, not the gross amount.

A certain amount of control can also be exercised by the Corporation for Public Broadcasting. All local stations rely on their annual Community Service Grants from the CPB as the bedrock of their revenues. Within the past two years the CPB has applied stiffer tests to new stations applying for CSGs. Stations must be able to demonstrate that they will service a significantly different audience from that served by an existing station in the same market; this may be evidenced either in terms of programming differentiation or in terms of audience differentiation, but it must be evidenced.

The CPB also has a certain amount of leeway in the annual review it conducts of grants to existing stations. In theory, at least, it would be possible for the CPB to insist on cooperative agreements being instituted between over-lapping stations. While the bulk of the Community Service Grants are "entitlements" for stations, there is also an incentive element that revolves around the definition of "public interest." If the CPB was to enforce a certain definition of public interest—one that would, for instance, enforce cooperative agreements between overlapping stations—the stations would doubtless object, but it is equal-ly likely that the Congress would eventually rule in the CPB's favor.

THE CORPORATION FOR PUBLIC BROADCASTING

Ever since its creation in 1968, the Corporation for Public Broadcasting has played a central yet often paradoxical role in the development of non-commercial television. Its responsibilities are not ambiguous, but they are often contradictory. As the principal regulatory body of public broadcasting, the CPB is accountable to the Congress, from which it receives its funding. But it is not a government agency. It was established as a private nonprofit corpora-tion for the very reason that it was intended to insulate public broadcasting from government influence. The 1967 Public Broadcasting Act laid down that the CPB "will not be an agency or establishment of the United States Government." Such good intentions were promptly minimized by the highly political nature of the process by which members of the board were to be appointed—fifteen members, all appointed by the president and confirmed by the Senate, not more than eight to be members of the same political party. Today there are only ten board members, and that (as a result of the 1992 Reauthorization Bill) will be reduced to nine in 1997 to avoid voting deadlocks.

At various times, the CPB has become heavily involved in program deci-sions. At other times (most notably in the past few years) it has gone to con-siderable lengths to distance itself from any kind of hands-on editorial involvement. The way the CPB has done this is by accepting what are virtu-ally formulas for the disbursement of most of its program money. About 60 per-cent of its total funds goes automatically to the local stations in the form of CSGs; of the $66 million that remains to be spent on television program-ming, half goes directly to the Chief Program Executive at PBS for national programming. Another portion is mandated by Congress to go to Independent Television Service (ITVS) programming ($7.5 million in 1991), and $5 mil-lion is contributed to the joint CPB/PBS Program Challenge Fund. There is not a great deal left for the CPB's Television Program Fund, and what there is is given in the form of grants to stations and independent producers submitting proposals.

All of which is fine, but the fact remains that the CPB is the regulatory body of public television and is responsible to Congress for the way its money is spent. The recent Senate debate on the Reauthorization Bill, and the amendments that were successfully attached to the bill, were evidence that not everyone is happy that the CPB has distanced itself so far from hands-on control. Some of the amendments were specifically designed to force the CPB to take a more active role. Among other things, they required the following:

♦ The CPB must review controversial programs after they have aired; in the event that any program is determined to have been one-sided, the CPB is required to provide funds to air the opposing viewpoint.

♦ The CPB must allow public comment to be submitted to it on the quality, creativity, diversity, balance and objectivity of national programs, and those comments must be distributed to all local stations.

♦ Fuller disclosure must be made of each program's funding in order to designate which programs are receiving taxpayer support. Files on programs that receive federal funding must be open to the public.

♦ "Indecent" programs must be restricted to broadcast between midnight and 6 A.M. (unless the station goes off the air at midnight, in which case 10 P.M. is the earliest broadcast time for such programs). This clause applies to commercial as well as noncommercial broadcasters and overtakes current FCC regulation allowing such programming between 8 P.M. and 6 A.M.

In themselves, these amendments amount to very little in the way of change for public television, but they can also be read as an invitation to the CPB to reassert its authority over programming. They are the result of lobbying by a persistent and powerful conservative consortium, assisted by even more powerful voices in the Congress and in the newspapers. These pressure groups are very unlikely to fade away.

The CPB was designed to be a regulator and a funding mechanism, as well as a promoter and encourager of creativity. "Heatshield" and "policeman" are words sometimes used to describe the CPB's role, but it is more complicated and more subtle than that. Speaking at the PBS annual meeting in June 1992, in the immediate aftermath of the Senate vote to authorize 1994–96 funding, Sheila Tate, chairman of the CPB board, said it was not the corporation's intention to "meddle" in programming content. "We will not attempt to stifle controversy," she said, but rather "attempt to create the opportunity for all reasonable, responsible voices to comment." Objectivity, balance, and fairness remain absolute requirements, but in monitoring them (and, where necessary, enforcing them) the CPB clearly does not wish to neuter the system. Public television was not invented to be bland: it was invented to be intelligent, thought-provoking, and (in the broadest sense of the word) educational. It is a delicate balance—one in which the CPB has a necessary but unenviable position.

The concentration of recent criticism on matters of political correctness has robbed the debate over the future of public television of what should have been much more important elements—questions of how public television can adapt itself to its new circumstances. These are the areas in which the CPB can, and must, exercise leadership in the next few years. It can promote and foster the development of electronic publishing within public television (especially within the educational sector); it can devise incentives (even, maybe, within the Community Service Grant formula) to enable stations to adapt to a new and expanding role within their communities; and it might even be the starting point for the creation of some sort of "model stations" program.

THE PUBLIC BROADCASTING SERVICE

PBS was invented in 1969 to operate the interconnection for the public television network because Congress did not want the CPB itself to operate it. PBS very quickly became the originator of the National Program Service and of many other program-related services to the stations. It is a private, non-profit corporation whose members are the 175 licensees that operate the 351 local stations. It is governed by a thirty-five-member board that includes sixteen lay representatives from stations' governing bodies, thirteen station managers, five general (or outside) directors, and the PBS president.

In the end, PBS is the servant of the stations; it is entirely subservient to their collective will. However, its focus is on national programming rather than on any one community; it therefore has a much wider perspective on the world and is capable of being a very uncomfortable partner to the stations. There is a tension in this relationship that is neither good nor bad; it is a fact of life.

Fundamentally, PBS is a democratic organization—the sum of its members. The major producing stations may have more influence than a tiny college station in the boondocks, but on matters of policy they each have one vote. There are highly radical stations and there are extremely conservative stations. There are stations licensed to constituencies as diverse as urban communities, state universities, and school boards. Yet they all manage to subsist under the one umbrella. What unites them is the need for a national schedule of quality programs. What often disunites them are their judgments of that schedule.

Putting national programming in the hands of a single program executive at PBS was a brave decision for the stations. It is an experiment that has received very mixed notices among the stations, but that was to be expected. What it comes down to in the end is not so much whether the system is an improvement on the Station Program Cooperative (SPC): It is, rather, whether the stations are prepared to put their fortunes so exclusively in the hands of so few people.

The acid test will probably be the marketplace: Is the CPE system going to deliver more members and more dollars to the stations? Preliminary estimates of viewer support in 1991 (the last year of the old SPC system, but the first year in which Jennifer Lawson and her colleagues were able to influence the content of continuing series and the day-to-day scheduling of the network) show that the number of members has gone down from 5.2 million to 5.1 million, but that the total dollars have risen from $272.5 million to $280.7 million. The years 1992 and 1993 (nonrecession years, and years in which the CPE can take much greater responsibility for the programming) will be better tests.

PBS is not itself a producing organization. It merely acquires programs, some from public television stations, some from independent producers, some from foreign producers. Most of these programs are commissioned by, and made for, public television; a minority of them are purchased "off the shelf."

In this respect public television is organized differently from public radio, and it is worth looking at the radio model to see if it holds lessons for television. American Public Radio (APR) is an independent, private, nonprofit program distribution company with more than 425 affiliate stations. National Public Radio (NPR), on the other hand, is a newsgathering, production, and program distribution company owned by public radio stations, most of whom are members of APR as well as NPR. NPR itself produces some of the most important programs in public radio, "Morning Edition" and "All Things Considered" being the most famous examples.

So the question is: Should PBS, or an offshoot of PBS, be in the production business? If PBS were to become a producer, it might supply local stations with a morning program to compete with the fare provided by the commercial networks. Or it might produce an early evening program that could be effectively "localized" by stations wishing to do so (by adding their own segments or their own presenters, in the way Group W's "PM/Evening Magazine" does in the commercial sector).

There are too few production centers for national programming at the moment. The burden of carrying the system rides on the backs of three or four stations. At various times it has been suggested that two, three, or even four national production centers might be established, geographically separate from one another so that East Coast stations would not have the predominate influence they have at the moment. But nothing has happened. The virtual disappearance of West Coast stations as major national producers in recent years has dramatized the problem.

Many people view any such proposals as dangerous. But something has to be done to address the problems of national programming, and not only in financial terms.

As long ago as 1978–79 Hartford Gunn, the greatest of PBS's innovators, designed a three-network system for national programming. The networks were designated by color. The Blue Service was the prime-time feed; the Green

Service was for "education for the home and school"; and the Red Service was to cater to "a multitude of special audiences" with programming "characterized by variety, local origin and diversity."[1] This three-network system was actually in operation at PBS for less than two years before it became a victim of the Reagan cutbacks.

Blue and Green survive to this day, though they are no longer called that. The Red Service, on the other hand, might easily have become redundant in the mid-1980s as cable channels came into being to serve the sort of niche audiences Gunn had in mind (C-SPAN and CNN/Headline News have certainly overtaken one of the most important of those areas). Nevertheless, if local stations are going to expand their services to communities in the next few years as fiber-optic delivery systems come into being, and if they are to avoid the problems of "overlapping," they will need more alternative programming from central and regional supply points.

There is, of course, an altogether contrary argument: concentrate on what you do best and do it better. Education and the prime-time scheduling remain the priorities of public television; that is where the resources and the effort must be directed. Leave the rest to the cable channels. But the acceptance of that argument depends on the role local stations are going to play. If they are to avoid becoming irrelevant, and if they are to build themselves into a powerful local resource, then they will need more support than they can currently expect from PBS (given PBS's very limited resources), and they will need a very radical change in the thinking by which they have traditionally been governed.

LOCAL STATIONS

It is necessary, first, to project forward to a time when the "last mile" problems that have dogged local stations have been overcome (and that time cannot be very far away—a decade, at most, hopefully less; in some areas of the country they have already been overcome). Second, one has to assume that the new technologies—video, computer, and satellite—will have come to dominate the requirements of education, as well as of many individual viewers. In these circumstances, the role of the local public television station *has* to change; terrestrial broadcasting may not be obsolete, but it long ago lost its primacy. Relevance is the criterion by which local stations should measure their future.

Public television stations were established for a number of different purposes. Look at the 175 licensees:

- Eighty-six are community organizations.

- Fifty-five are colleges or universities.

◆   Twenty-three are statewide authorities.

◆   Eleven are local educational or municipal authorities.

Each of these groups has a different mission; and within each there are geographic and demographic differences that dictate different priorities and different methods. But the stations in these groups have four basic functions in common:

◆   They receive the satellite feeds of national and instructional programming and relay them to homes, schools, and institutions in their own localities.

◆   They adapt (and, if necessary, add to) the national schedules in order to suit local needs.

◆   They raise funds within their communities to support their own station in particular, and public television in general.

◆   They provide an array of services to their own community, ranging from local program production, to educational services, to outreach activities.

The first of these functions has traditionally meant signal delivery. It is going to have to be redefined as *program* delivery—sometimes by cable, sometimes on video cassette or disc, sometimes in the form of computer software or CD-ROM, occasionally over the air (and then, very often, by facilitating direct satellite links).

No one can argue with the stations about the second function— rescheduling the national feeds and purchasing substitute programming— because the money they use to do it is entirely their own and because only they can truly judge their local requirements. Nevertheless, it cannot pass unremarked that this function (according to the BCG study) costs $100 million a year, which is about 20 percent more than the stations jointly contribute to the national program budget.

The third function—fundraising—depends on how effectively the other functions are performed, but most especially it depends on the national program schedule. It ought also to be assessed as a net figure rather than as a gross figure.

Which leaves the real problem area—local presence and local programming. The public television station of the 1990s must be more than just a local transmitter. The role it assumes will depend on its geographic location and the nature of its licensee. But every station is, in itself, a telecommunications instrument. Its job is to put that instrument to the service of the community.

For some stations (particularly those in the inner city) this may mean playing a very active role, allowing the station to be used as a catalyst for change. For others (in more rural areas) it may mean developing and expanding the traditional role as a public telecommunications hub, serving the community and its agencies as a supplier and distributor of educational resources and high-quality programming. For yet others (particularly those licensed to educational institutions) it may mean concentrating exclusively on the original brief—"ETV."

Various scenarios are being developed within public television to perform these roles in the changing environment of the 1990s. "The public telecommunication complex," "the electronic public library," and "the electronic town square" are three such scenarios, not mutually exclusive. They seek to bring public television squarely into the world of the new technologies, to fit the educational requirements of the present and the future (so far as they can be seen), and to differentiate public television stations, and the role they play in their communities, from their commercial brethren (which is important). None of these scenarios are likely to be sufficient in themselves; stations will wish to adapt them to suit the needs of their own individual missions.

At the same time, none of them dictates that stations have to originate their own local broadcast programming. Some stations will continue to do so, some probably should not. It is an expensive activity and one that has been somewhat emasculated by budget cuts in recent years. Public television is not known for its local programming, except in a very few communities, whereas it *is* known for its national programming. Nevertheless, where it clearly serves the local mission, and where it can be done professionally, local programming will be an important ingredient.

There are stations with distinctive voices serving distinctive communities, there are statewide systems providing a service that is not offered by commercial stations, and there are inner-city stations that play a significant part in the lives of their communities; all these would naturally want to originate local programs as part of their functions. The Nitty Gritty City Group is just one example. Formed in 1989, it consists of fifteen urban stations that have pooled their resources in order to test the hypothesis that public television stations can contribute to problem solving in the inner cities. The stations share experiences and use their airtime and facilities to develop solutions to some of the more intractable problems of the cities. "Street Watch," for instance, is a series that looks at inner-city problems (the homeless, gangs, drugs, and so on), examining and comparing ways in which the fifteen different cities have set out to tackle them. These are broadcast programs, but they are accompanied by closed-circuit teleconference workshops that bring together the participating networks from the fifteen cities to discuss their different approaches.

Commercial broadcasters are by no means the enemy. One of the essential ingredients of the library model—or any other model that is devised for public television stations in the future—is cooperation with commercial stations. It already happens in some areas. WTVS, Detroit, for instance, shares with the city's commercial stations a series called "City of Youth": nine separate programs examining the future of children in the city have been broadcast simultaneously by seven stations. They achieved a 52 share.

There are many other ways in which local programming can contribute to a station's mission, but its costs (and those of the necessary facilities and hardware) have to be weighed against the effectiveness of other, nonbroadcast, activities and services. Above all, there is no point in competing in the broadcast market unless a station can look professional on the air. The most frequent (and probably the most damaging) accusation made against public television stations is that some of them look amateurish. Nowhere does that apply more than to pledge programs. Another priority of the stations must therefore be to lessen the amount of on-screen time taken up with fundraising and to increase the amount of effort devoted to off-screen fundraising.

One veteran station manager has described the atmosphere in public television as "polite anarchy." Every station jealously guards its independence from the center, and from most other stations as well. Each exists within its own community, and most of them are unwilling to look much beyond unless it is to criticize other elements of the "system."

"Entitlement" has become an all too common watchword among the stations— entitlement to Community Service Grants from the CPB, entitlement to contribute minimally to national programming, entitlement to act independently of the rest of the system whenever it suits them. All these are, of course, just that: entitlements of the stations. It is the stations that hold the licenses to broadcast. Given that they observe the necessary FCC and CPB regulations, they are entitled to spend their money in any way they see fit. It is not quite true to say that they are sovereign (except on their own airwaves), but it is almost certainly true that no substantive changes in the organization and structure of public television can be made without their concurrence.

When one looks back over the twenty-five-year history of public television in this country, it is striking how much attention has been given (and still is) to the central institutions, the CPB and PBS, and how little attention has been paid to the needs of the biggest players (and the biggest spenders) in the system, the local stations. Between 1951 and the early 1970s, the Ford Foundation breathed life into national programming. There are those who think that a similar (but less costly) initiative is required in the 1990s, but this time it should be devoted entirely to addressing the local problems of public television. With or without such an initiative, an awful lot hinges on the stations' ability to adapt to the new circumstances.

◆ ◆ ◆ ◆

None of this is to minimize the problems highlighted by the recent congressional debates. Those problems—accountability, bias, use of taxpayer money—need to be addressed every day by public broadcasters. They will certainly be addressed by legislators the next time federal funding is an issue. This paper has tried to show that there are other, less publicized but even more fundamental, problems in public television. They are problems of mission, relevance, and the use of resources. How can public television, as an educational resource, remain relevant to the changing needs of teachers and students? How can local stations adapt to the new technologies and the new environment in which they find themselves? How can national programming be financed and expanded to cope with the increasing competition of cable channels and other sources of programming?

These (and one could add to the list) are very basic questions. The ways in which they are answered will determine the relevance and importance of public television in the twenty-first century.

NOTES

INTRODUCTION

1. Willard D. Rowland, Jr., "The Case of the United States: A History and Analysis of Public Service Broadcasting in the United States—Its Mandate, Institutions, and Conflicts," in Robert K. Avery, ed., *Public Broadcasting in a Multichannel Environment* (White Plains, N.Y.: Longman, in press).

2. Public Broadcasting Service, *Funding the Vision* (September 1991).

3. Project Paper No. 10 of the System Planning Project, from the office of Hartford N. Gunn, Jr., Vice Chairman of the Public Broadcasting System (Public Broadcasting Service, May 23, 1979).

4. Willard D. Rowland, Jr., "The Case of the United States."

CHAPTER ONE

1. Carnegie Commission on Educational Television, *Public Television: A Program for Action* (New York: Harper and Row, 1967), recommendation no. 10.

2. Ibid., recommendation no. 11.

3. Carnegie Commission on the Future of Public Broadcasting, *A Public Trust: The Report of the Carnegie Commission on the Future of Public Broadcasting* (New York: Bantam Books, 1979), p. 43n.

4. "Resolution of the Board of Directors" (Owings Mills, Md.: Corporation for Public Broadcasting, January 10, 1973).

5. Carnegie Commission on the Future of Public Broadcasting, *A Public Trust*, p. 50.

6. Ibid., p. 14.

7. Willard D. Rowland, Jr., "The Case of the United States."

8. *Broadcasting*, November 1991.

CHAPTER TWO

1. Marc Doyle, *The Future of Television* (Lincolnwood, Ill.: NTC Publishing Group, 1992), p. 158.

CHAPTER THREE

1. Taken from a list of goals circulated at the education summit arranged by the White House and National Governors' Association and held at the University of Virginia in Charlottesville, September 27–28, 1989.

CHAPTER FOUR

1. Senate Committee on Commerce, Science, and Transportation, *Public Telecommunications Act of 1988: Report of the Senate Committee on Commerce, Science, and Transportation* (Washington, D.C.: Government Printing Office, 1988).
2. Ibid.
3. Summarized from The Boston Consulting Group, *Strategies for Public Television in a Multi-Channel Environment* (Corporation for Public Broadcasting, March 1991), The User's Guide section, pp. 15–20.
4. Alvin H. Perlmutter, Inc., *The Voters' Channel: A Feasibility Study* (The John and Mary Markle Foundation, June 1990).
5. Ibid.
6. S. Robert Lichter, Daniel Amundsom, and Linda A. Lichter, *Balance and Diversity in PBS Documentaries* (Center for Media and Public Affairs, March 1992).

CHAPTER FIVE

1. *CPB Policy Development and Planning* (Corporation for Pubilc Broadcasting, July 1991).
2. "Making Public Television Public," *The Heritage Foundation Backgrounder*, no. 873, January 18, 1992.
3. *The Credit You Deserve: A Guide to Your Public Television On-Air Credit* (Public Broadcasting Service, 1989), a pamphlet distributed by PBS to corporations and potential underwriters.

CHAPTER SIX

1. From the office of Hartford N. Gunn, Jr., Vice Chairman of the Public Broadcasting System, Project Paper no. 7 of the System Planning Project (Public Broadcasting Service, May 4, 1979).

INDEX

ABOUT THE AUTHOR

R ichard Somerset-Ward was on the staff of the British Broadcasting
Corporation for twenty-one years, serving most recently as Head of Music
and Arts Programming for BBC Television as well as BBC's Director in the
United States. Since 1984, he has run his own independent company, RSW
Enterprises, specializing in international media and international coproduction.